THE
METAPHYSICAL BASIS
OF
PLATO'S ETHICS

BY

ARTHUR BERNARD COOK M.A.

FELLOW OF TRINITY COLLEGE CAMBRIDGE

"Quis ille primus, cuius ex imagine
Natura solers finxit humanum genus,
Aeternus, incorruptus, aequaevus polo,
Unusque et universus, exemplar Dei?"—
MILTON

Cambridge
DEIGHTON BELL & CO.
London GEORGE BELL & SONS
1895

CAMBRIDGE
PRINTED BY JONATHAN PALMER
ALEXANDRA STREET

CONTENTS

	PAGE
PREFACE	ix
PART I. THE PLATONIC THEORY OF MIND	1
§ 1. The *Parmenides*	1
§ 2. The *Sophist*	17
§ 3. Aristotle's *Psychology*	23
PART II. HIGHER AND LOWER MENTALITY	54
§ 1. Purpose and Necessity	55
§ 2. Identity and Difference	68
§ 3. Theology	85
PART III. METAPHYSICAL DESCENT AND MORAL ASCENT.	113
INDEX LOCORUM	153

PREFACE

Τί οὖν ἡμεῖς ἐροῦμεν ἐπὶ τοσούτοις καὶ τοιούτοις ἐξηγηταῖς τοῦ Πλάτωνος; καὶ τί προσθήσομεν ἐκ τῆς ἡμετέρας ἑστίας;

PROKLOS *in Parm.* ed. Cousin vi. 30.

THE following essay is neither a systematic account of Plato's metaphysics, nor an adequate exposition of Plato's ethics. Its scope is a narrower one. It aims at clearing up the connection between the two. And, if the attempt has led me to reinterpret the metaphysical scheme that underlay the ethics of matured Platonism, my purpose throughout has been to show how intimately—and indeed vitally—the latter was connected with the former. Thus far at least I find myself in accordance with the general tendency of modern Platonic criticism. For the supposed independence, not to say antagonism, of the several parts of Plato's philosophy, which still mars the work of certain exponents, is nowadays falling into disrepute. We are beginning to look askance on all constructions involving the philosopher in incongruous positions. And this is due partly, I think, to a growing appreciation of the artistic side of his thought, partly to special efforts that have been made to determine from theoretical content or linguistic style the true order of the Platonic writings. The former movement postulates that here, if anywhere, a speculative system must mean a harmonious whole; the latter has shown that sundry seeming inconsistencies are but tide-marks of a progressive development. But, whatever be the precise causes which have of recent times tended to discredit the patchwork Platonism of the past, it will fairly be demanded of any fresh endeavour to articulate the Idealist doctrine that it represent that doctrine as an organic unity.

This being admitted, the only safe course is to regard the Platonic philosophy from the standpoint of some ὅρος ὁρισθεὶς μέγας for which Plato is himself responsible. Now of all such ὅροι that which is most constantly affirmed and most jealously guarded is the reality of the Ideal world. The late Dr. Maguire has somewhere said that "the objectivity of the Idea is the corner-stone of Platonism." I should prefer to substitute the term "reality" as a translation of οὐσία, because the cardinal dogma of the *Timaeus* asserts that the nature of οὐσία is to be at once ταὐτὸν and θάτερον, *i.e.* not only objective but also subjective. And here it may conduce to clearness if, by way of preamble, I sketch the main drift of my essay, indicating in the briefest possible manner how this theory of objective and subjective οὐσία furnished a satisfactory foundation for the superstructure of morality.

Plato conceived the universe to be a νοητὸν ζῷον containing within itself a series of νοητὰ ζῷα. Every such ζῷον, whether supreme or subordinate,—if it is to make good its claim to real being—must (he says) pass from the objective phase of self-identity into the subjective phase of self-differentiation. The former state consists in the intuitional exercise of pure thought; the latter comprises the emotive presentations of knowledge, opinion, sensation. But the passage from the one to the other is a necessary feature of each and every νοητὸν ζῷον. As regards nomenclature,—the supreme ζῷον in its higher condition is the sovereign Mind; in its lower condition it is the θεοὶ θεῶν. The subordinate ζῷα in their higher condition are the Ideas, in their lower condition they are particular specimens of the natural kinds. And since the higher mentality must be deemed superhuman, Plato calls the sovereign Mind θεὸς and the Ideas ἀΐδιοι θεοί, in contradistinction to particulars which are at best only δαίμονες.

The significance of these remarks will be at once apparent if we consider the case of a single νοητὸν ζῷον—say that of Man. Man being one of the subordinate ζῷα expresses one aspect, viz. the humanity, of the supreme ζῷον. He is endowed with four faculties, named respectively νοῦς, and ἐπιστήμη, δόξα, αἴσθησις. As possessed of νοῦς he is the Idea of Man, an immutable entity correlating with, i.e. thinking and thought by, all entities of the same order. As possessed of ἐπιστήμη, δόξα, αἴσθησις, Man lapses from permanent thought into transient knowledge, opinion, sensation,—no longer functioning as a unitary Ideal Mind, but as an indefinite plurality of particular minds. These particulars in their turn correlate with, i.e. apprehend and are apprehended by, particulars of all the νοητὰ ζῷα: as actively apprehensive we call them ψυχαί, as passively apprehensible we call them σώματα.

Further, the world of absolute being (the sovereign Mind + the Ideal Minds) is termed a παράδειγμα, whose εἰκών is the world of relative becoming (the starry gods + all specimens of the natural kinds). And just as metaphysics insists that the former must pass into the latter, so morality demands that the latter—to the best of their ability—must return towards the former. But since the Ideal Minds are partial and serial determinations of the sovereign Mind, this demand of conformity to their appropriate Ideas implies the desirability of attaining, so far as may be, to the condition of the sovereign Mind itself. Such attainment in the present life is perforce meagre and limited; but the theory of transmigration hereafter opens up possibilities beyond compute. In fine, the ethical end for particulars as determined by Plato's ontology is to minimise the difference between their own psychosis and that of the supreme θεός— a quest which leads them through the successive stages of the Ideal series.

The discussion of the system here summarised has fallen into three divisions. The first educes the main outlines from a consideration of certain passages of importance in the Dialogues and elsewhere. The second emphasises the distinction between the realm of objective being and the realm of subjective becoming. The third states the metaphysical view of the latter as a copy of the former, and endeavours to show how that view impliedly inculcates the rational treatment of individual souls and bodies in accordance with the ethical end above mentioned.

It will be seen from this statement that my obligations to Cambridge teaching are not slight. Dr. Jackson's papers in the *Journal of Philology* (vols. x—xv) have, to my thinking, established beyond reasonable doubt the chronology of the more important Dialogues. Any attempt to reconstruct Plato's mature Idealism must henceforward be based mainly upon the *Philebus*, the *Parmenides*, the *Theaetetus*, the *Sophist*, the *Politicus*, the *Timaeus*, and the *Laws*. And those who set about it may spare themselves the burden of proving "(1) a revision of the list of Ideas, whereby relations, negations, and artificial products ceased to be regarded as Ideas proper (αὐτὰ καθ' αὐτὰ εἴδη); and (2) a modification of the conception of the relation subsisting between the Idea and its particulars, whereby for 'participation' (μέθεξις) of the latter in the former was substituted 'imitation' (μίμησις)." Again, Mr. Archer-Hind's interpretation of the *Timaeus* proves to all who have ears to hear that, according to Plato's esoteric meaning, "the one universal Thought evolves itself into a multitude of finite intelligences, which are so constituted as to apprehend not only by pure reason, but also by what we call the senses, with all their attendant subjective phenomena of time and space."

If in some points of moment I have ventured to dissent from those who propounded these weighty opinions, it is because I cannot but pursue to the end the principle that the Ideal world is composed of ὄντα, understanding by the word οὐσία in every case a combination of objective with subjective thought. One great outcome of that principle has, I believe, been hitherto overlooked: I mean the fact that for Plato the unit of metaphysical and ethical measurement is neither the Idea nor the individual, but the νοητὸν ζῷον—a personal being whose intellectual activity comprises the two essentials of "reality," namely the unitary νόησις of the Idea and the diffracted γνῶσις of its particulars. To press the consequences of this fundamental doctrine seemed to me not only legitimate, but necessary.

TRINITY COLLEGE, CAMBRIDGE,
July 8th, 1895.

PART I.

THE PLATONIC THEORY OF MIND

Before the ethical bearings of Plato's Idealism can be appreciated, it is of primary importance to determine the relation in which the Ideas themselves stand towards Mind. This relation—essential as it is to a sound understanding of the Platonic system—is nowhere explicitly set forth in the extant dialogues. Their author has *more suo* left it to be inferred either from the necessary presuppositions of certain broad tenets, or from a few incidental passages of pregnant meaning. The former, among which may be mentioned the doctrines of Metempsychosis and Anamnesis, will be more conveniently dealt with at a later stage of the present argument. The latter call for immediate analysis, as enabling us to formulate simply and directly the connection which we seek to ascertain.

§ I. *The Parmenides.*

In *Parm.* 132 B *seq.* the Platonic Sokrates, wishing to secure the unity of the Idea against the criticism of the Platonic Parmenides, suggests that perhaps each Idea is a thought (νόημα) existent only in souls (ἐν ψυχαῖς). To this suggestion Parmenides retorts:

(i) That a νόημα must have a content, an ὄν τι; and that the content which this νόημα νοεῖ will be the Idea as previously described and therefore as previously refuted.

(ii) That if on the one hand each Idea is a νόημα, and on the other hand particulars are related to Ideas by participation (μέθεξις), then particulars—as aggregates of immanent Ideas—may be said to consist ἐκ νοημάτων, in fact to be themselves νοήματα, objects of pure thought. Hence follows one of two alternatives: either (a) all particulars are νοοῦντα, or (b) some particulars are not νοοῦντα, in spite of their being νοήματα.[1]

---

[1] I understand νοήματα ὄντα ἀνόητα εἶναι (*Parm.* 132 C) as spoken of *particulars*; for, if a thing ἐκ νοημάτων ἐστίν, it is—to borrow a phrase of Aristotle's—σύνθεσίς τις ἤδη νοημάτων ὥσπερ ἐν ὄντων, and may justly be described as itself a νόημα. Another logically correct interpretation of the second limb of the dilemma would be: "or there are some *Ideal* νοήματα which are not contained in minds" But this seems to me inadmissible on two grammatical grounds: (1) It involves a somewhat awkward change of subject from πάντα = *particulars* to νοήματα = *Ideas*; (2) the word ἀνόητος is elsewhere used in a passive sense only when passivity is distinctly suggested by the context (e.g. *h. hom. Merc.* 80 ἄφραστ' ἠδ' ἀνόητα διέπλεκε θαυματὰ ἔργα, Parm. ed. R. and P. v. 73 τὴν μὲν ἐᾶν ἀνόητον, ἀνώνυμον, Plat. *Phaedo* 80 B τῷ μέν . . . νοητῷ καὶ μονοειδεῖ καὶ ἀδιαλύτῳ . . . τῷ δὲ . . . ἀνοήτῳ καὶ πολυειδεῖ καὶ διαλυτῷ, Dionys. Areop. *de div. nom.* c. 1 ὑπερούσιος

To put the dilemma in other words. If we choose the first horn (*a*), we assume that νοήματα (*i.e.* particulars, regarded as aggregates of Ideas) must in every case possess the power of thinking; and thereby we contradict common sense, which affirms that *e.g.* a palm-tree cannot think. If we choose the second horn (*b*), we hold that common sense is right in declaring *e.g.* a palm-tree to be ἀνόητον; and thereby we deny the assumption that would equate all νοήματα (*i.e.* particulars, regarded as aggregates of Ideas) with νοοῦντα.

Now this argument as a whole turns on the acceptance of the equation between νόημα and νοοῦν. For the wording of the first alternative—ἢ δοκεῖν σοι ἐκ νοημάτων ἕκαστον εἶναι καὶ πάντα νοεῖν—clearly implies that πάντα νοεῖν is the natural consequence of ἐκ νοημάτων ἕκαστον εἶναι. And the second alternative offers no difficulty at all, unless we are convinced that every νόημα must be a νοοῦν: that it does offer difficulty is shown by Sokrates' answer—'Ἀλλ' οὐδὲ τοῦτο, φάναι, ἔχει λόγον. Again, it is noteworthy that in Parmenides' first retort the same postulate was

---

οὐσία καὶ νοῦς ἀνόητος καὶ λόγος ἄρρητος), and not always then (*e.g.* [Alex.] *in Arist. Met.* ed. Hayduck p. 670, 27 τὴν γὰρ νοητὴν καὶ θείαν πολλοὶ μὴ εἶναι ἀνοήτως ἀπεφήναντο). In view of these objections I have followed a simpler syntax, and given to ἀνόητος a meaning that Stephanus calls "frequentissimum et passim obvium" (*e.g.* Plat. *Tim.* 30 B, where, as in *Gorg.* 514 C, ἀνόητος is opposed to νοῦν ἔχων).

tacitly made by the words—Οὐχ ἑνός τινος, ὃ ἐπὶ πᾶσιν ἐκεῖνο τὸ νόημα ἐπὸν νοεῖ, μίαν τινὰ οὖσαν ἰδέαν; In short, both the language of the first retort and the fact that the second is couched in the form of a dilemma lead us to suppose that the Platonic Sokrates and his critic were alike prepared to maintain that *every νόημα must be a νοοῦν*.

Whether this assumption is an axiom or a paradox will depend upon the exact significance that we attribute to νόημα. As with our own word "thought," so in the case of νόημα it is possible to distinguish a variety of allied meanings. Proklos *in Parm.* ed. Cousin v. 147 observes λέγεται γὰρ νόημα καὶ τὸ νοητὸν αὐτὸ τὸ νοηθὲν καὶ τὸ ἐνέργημα καὶ τὸ γνωστικὸν τοῦ νοοῦντος, *i.e.* the term νόημα is applied (1) to the actual object of thought, the thing thought of; (2) to the process of thinking, or more strictly to that process as exemplified on any definite occasion; (3) to the cognitive faculty of the thinker. If in the passage with which we are concerned νόημα bears this *third* sense, then the statement νόημα νοεῖ is self-evident, and further enquiry is futile. But the usage of νόημα to denote the "cognitive faculty" is poetical, as may be seen from the *lexica*[2]; and at this juncture, where much may hinge on the right selection of a single word, a

---

[2] *e.g.* Hom. *Od.* 215, Hes. *Op.* 129, *Theog.* 656, Empedocl. ed. Karsten vv. 313, 316, 317.

poet's licence would be utterly out of place. Had Plato meant "the thinker" or "the thinking faculty," he would assuredly have used τὸ νοοῦν or ὁ νοῦς. Can it be then that νόημα here bears its *second* meaning, and denotes "a process of thinking"? Two objections at once suggest themselves. In the first place, if A thinks B, it is fair to describe A or A's mind as thinking; it may also be fair to presume that B or B's mind has a similar faculty for thought; but is it fair to say that A's thinking thinks? Has the expression νόημα νοεῖ thus interpreted any intelligible meaning? And in the second place, if we grant that by a laxity of phraseology such a statement might be made[3], it must be admitted that νόημα thus becomes the equivalent of νόησις. But it is difficult to believe that for a common and straightforward term Plato would have substituted a comparatively rare and ambiguous one.[4] A glance at Ast's *Lexicon* will

---

[3] The elasticity of the English language tolerates the following sentence: "If the passing thought be the directly verifiable existent, which no school has hitherto doubted it to be, then *that thought is itself the thinker*, and psychology need not look beyond" (W. James, *The Principles of Psychology*, i. 401, cp. 369). The nearest approach to this that I know of in Greek is a clause quoted by Stephanus *s.v.* νοερός: "Mire cum νόημα conjungit Niceph. Callist. H. E. vol. i p 8 B, ἵν' ᾖ σοι μὲν καὶ ὁ νοῦς . . . ἀθόλωτος, βρύων νοερὰ καὶ θεῖα νοήματα." But Byzantine bombast is foreign to the *Parmenides*.

[4] It might be argued, on the strength of Arist. *Psych.* A. 3. 13. 407 a 7 ἡ δὲ νόησις τὰ νοήματα, that νοήματα is used as the plural of νόησις. But (1) in that passage "thought is thoughts" means that the

show that, as compared with νόησις, νόημα occurs but seldom in the Platonic writings. Discounting *Meno* 95 E, *Soph.* 237 A, 258 D, as quotations and *Symp.* 197 E, an avowedly poetical passage in Agathon's speech, we meet with it again only in *Politicus* 260 D, where heralds as a class are said to issue commands ἀλλότρια νοήματα παραδεχόμενον. The word is apposite there just because it has not a subjective but an objective value—the king entrusts his νόημα to the herald, as the manufacturer hands over his wares to the retail dealer. It appears to me certain, therefore, that in the present passage also νόημα is used in the *first* of the three senses enumerated by Proklos. It denotes "the actual object of thought, the thing thought of." We may still, however, raise the question whether νόημα means (*a*) the object thought of, as it is independently of the thinking subject, or (*b*) the object thought of, as represented by the thinking subject to his own mind. The former, to speak with all accuracy, is τὸ νοητὸν or τὸ νοούμενον, "that which can be" or "that which actually is appre-

---

mental activity of the thinking subject consists in representations of objects thought, not merely in repeated exhibitions of itself: where the process of thinking is entirely self-contained, ἔστιν ἡ νόησις νοήσεως νόησις, not νοήματος or νοημάτων νόησις; (2) the plural νοήσεις was available. To Arist. *Probl. IH.* 7. 917 *a* 39 (quoted by L. & S.) and Plut. *Mor.* 691 C, 1120 A (quoted by Stephanus) add Porphyr. *Op.* ed. Holsten p. 66 εἰς δὲ ἑαυτὴν εἰσιοῦσα πρὸς τὸν νοῦν ἐν ταῖς νοήσεσι γίγνεται (*sc.* ἡ ψυχή) . . . καὶ αἱ νοήσεις οὐκ ἄνευ φαντασίας.

hended by thought." The latter is τὸ νόημα. Thus Plutarch *de placit. phil.* iv. 11 says ἔστι δὲ νόημα φάντασμα[5] διανοίας λογικοῦ ζώου—a definition elsewhere used to elucidate the Stoic term λεκτόν, which also was the mental representation of τὸ σημαινόμενον. This distinction between (*a*) τὸ νοούμενον and (*b*) τὸ νοούμενον ᾖ νοούμενον would be important enough if we were dealing with objects sensibly perceived But in the case of the Platonic Ideas it does not trouble us, because—as Proklos, *ibid* 140, puts it—ὁ Σωκράτης ἐν νοήμασι τισὶν οὐσιῶσθαι τὰς ἰδέας ὑπέλαβεν.[6] The Idea and Mind's thought of the Idea are one. The former has no existence apart from the latter We have mounted to a level where the word φάντασμα, in so far as it implies the low ground of sense-perception, is not applicable,—a level where less venturesome theorists are not likely to linger: Arist. *Psych.* Γ. 3. 8. 432 *a* 12 τὰ δὲ πρῶτα νοήματα τίνι διοίσει τοῦ μὴ φαντάσματα εἶναι ; ἢ οὐδὲ τἆλλα φαντάσματα, ἀλλ' οὐκ ἄνευ φαντασμάτων. I conclude,

---

[5] Cp. Alex. *de anim.* ed. Bruns p. 85, 20 ἐγγίνεται δὲ ἡ τοιάδε ἕξις τῷ νῷ τὴν ἀρχὴν κατὰ μετάβασιν ἀπὸ τῆς περὶ τὰ αἰσθητὰ συνεχοῦς ἐνεργείας ὥσπερ ὄψιν τινὰ ἀπ' αὐτῶν λαμβάνοντος τοῦ καθόλου θεωρητικήν, ὃ κατ' ἀρχὰς μὲν νόημα καὶ ἔννοια καλεῖται, πλεονάσαν δὲ καὶ ποικίλον καὶ πολύτροπον γινόμενον, ὡς δύνασθαι καὶ χωρὶς τῆς αἰσθητικῆς ὑποβάθρας ποιεῖν τοῦτο, νοῦς ἤδη.

[6] Cp. Alex. *in Arist. Met* ed. Hayduck p. 92, 19, 22, ἐν τῷ νοεῖσθαι ἰδέαις ἡ ὑπόστασις and τὸ εἶναι αὐτῶν ἐν τῷ νοεῖσθαι.

then, that the meaning of νόημα as it occurs in this section of the *Parmenides* may be satisfactorily defined as "the object of thought" without further qualification. And it is of such a νόημα that the interlocutors assume what is by no means a truism, viz. that it possesses the power of thinking.

We set out, then, impressed with the belief that a νόημα has a capacity for νόησις, and furnished with Sokrates' suggestion that each Idea is a νόημα. We are, however, hampered by the difficulty which Parmenides urged in the first horn of the dilemma, viz., that if the Idea is a νόημα, and *if particulars may be said* τῶν εἰδῶν μετέχειν, particulars too consist ἐκ νοημάτων—in fact, are νοήματα; and therefore particulars ought always to be νοοῦντα—a result which is disproved by experience. This difficulty vanishes with the surrender of the immanence of the Ideas. Sokrates now declares that the μέθεξις is οὐκ ἄλλη τις ἢ εἰκασθῆναι αὐτοῖς (*Parm.* 132 D). Hence particulars are no longer made up of νοήματα in such a way as to be themselves the objects of pure thought; rather they should be described as ὁμοιώματα or μιμήματα of the Ideas. It follows—or would follow, if the conversation did not take another turn—that a particular as such is incapable of νόησις, and we escape the paradoxical conclusion that *e.g.* a palm-tree has the faculty of thought; indeed, we confine these νοήματα νοοῦντα to the world of Ideas.

OF PLATO'S ETHICS. 9

Having surmounted this obstacle, we reconnoitre our position. Two principles of importance have been deliberately admitted :—

Firstly, in every instance of νόησις the νοούμενον must be a single real existence, an ὄν τι.

Secondly, all νοήματα have a capacity for νόησις.

The Idea, then, on this showing (i) is a really existent unit. Consequently it will be possessed of such properties and subject to such conditions as may hereafter be proved essential to οὐσία. (ii) It is a thought that thinks. Now to the question, "What does it think?" we can but reply, "Thoughts." And since every νόημα is a νοοῦν, our answer means "Thoughts that think." Moreover, as we have confined "Thoughts that think" to the world of Ideas, we are now asserting that any given Idea thinks Ideas. Thus the Ideal series, as at present conceived, consists in certain νοήματα νοοῦντα which think themselves[7] and one another,[8]—the range of

---

[7] Note that, when Sokrates answers in the affirmative the question, Οὐχ ἑνός τινος, ὃ ἐπὶ πᾶσιν ἐκεῖνο τὸ νόημα ἐπὸν νοεῖ, μίαν τινὰ οὖσαν ἰδέαν, (*Parm.* 132 C), it is not to the conception of the Idea thinking itself that Parmenides demurs, but to the reappearance of the Idea as previously defined with all its former disabilities.

[8] In *Phaedrus* 247 C, D, soul is described as an οὐσία ὄντως . . . μόνῳ θεατὴ νῷ. Of this intelligible entity it is said : καθορᾷ μὲν αὐτὴν δικαιοσύνην, καθορᾷ δὲ σωφροσύνην, καθορᾷ δὲ ἐπιστήμην, οὐχ ᾗ γένεσις πρόσεστιν . . . ἀλλὰ τὴν ἐν τῷ ὅ ἐστιν ὂν ὄντως ἐπιστήμην οὖσαν· καὶ τἆλλα ὡσαύτως τὰ ὄντα ὄντως θεασαμένη κ.τ.λ. *Mutatis mutandis* this passage is applicable to the Idea as it is portrayed in the *Parmenides*.

this mental activity being exclusively restricted to the domain of Ideal truth:

> *Parm.* 134 A Οὐκοῦν καὶ ἐπιστήμη, φάναι, αὐτὴ μὲν ὃ ἔστιν ἐπιστήμη, τῆς ὃ ἔστιν ἀλήθεια, αὐτῆς ἂν ἐκείνης εἴη ἐπιστήμη ; Πάνυ γε. Ἑκάστη δὲ αὖ τῶν ἐπιστημῶν ἣ ἔστιν, ἑκάστου τῶν ὄντων, ὃ ἔστιν, εἴη ἂν ἐπιστήμη· ἢ οὔ ; Ναί.

Let us here pause to enquire from what sources these fundamental doctrines derive. The conviction that every *νόημα* must be a *νοοῦν* might *primâ facie* be ranged under the general belief that "like is known by like," appeal being made to Plato's earlier utterance:—*Phaedo* 80 A, B. τάδε ἡμῖν ξυμβαίνει, τῷ μὲν θείῳ καὶ ἀθανάτῳ καὶ νοητῷ ... ὁμοιότατον εἶναι ψυχήν. For if the soul resembles intelligibles, intelligibles presumably resemble the soul. But it is one thing to assert that the object of thought is incorporeal (even the Stoics went thus far), and another thing to hold that the thoughts of the thinking soul must be themselves capable of thinking. This latter creed was apparently based on the authority of the historical Parmenides, from whose poem two passages may be cited as illustrative of the point. The first of these (ed. R. and P. vv. 39—40) is

> οὔτε γὰρ ἂν γνοίης τό γε μὴ ἐόν, οὐ γὰρ ἀνυστόν,
> οὔτε φράσαις· τὸ γὰρ αὐτὸ νοεῖν ἔστιν τε καὶ εἶναι.

The general[9] sense of the last clause is "We can think only of what exists;" and the argument shows that, if we can think of nothing but τὸ ὄν, τὸ μὴ ὂν will be both unknowable and unspeakable. In fact, Parmenides held that every thought has a truly existent content, inasmuch as τὸ νοούμενον *must ever be* τὸ ὄν. And this is just what the Platonic Parmenides urges in his first retort to Sokrates' tentative reconstruction:

Parm. 132 B τί οὖν, φάναι, ἓν ἕκαστόν ἐστι τῶν νοημάτων, νόημα δὲ οὐδενός; Ἀλλ' ἀδύνατον, εἰπεῖν. Ἀλλὰ τινός; Ναί. Ὄντος ἢ οὐκ ὄντος; Ὄντος.

The second passage to which I allude is (ed. R. and P. vv. 94—96)

τωὐτὸν δ' ἐστὶ νοεῖν τε καὶ οὕνεκέν ἐστι νόημα·
οὐ γὰρ ἄνευ τοῦ ἐόντος, ἐν ᾧ πεφατισμένον ἐστίν,
εὑρήσεις τὸ νοεῖν.

The argument here may be thus paraphrased,—

You do not find thought apart from τὸ ὄν, wherein thought finds its expression:

[You do not find thought's object apart from τὸ ὄν:]

---

[9] Literally, the words may be rendered "The same thing exists both for thinking and for being" (*Datival Infinitive*): or possibly, giving to ἐστιν its technical meaning = "*It* is," we should translate "*It* is the same both for thinking and for being."

Ergo thought and thought's object are co-extensive[10]—both are τὸ ὄν.

It will be observed that the two passages are complementary. The minor premiss, which is wanting in the second, is exactly supplied by the first. The argument as a whole, led to the simple corollary that, if thought coincides with thought's object, that object may be said to think.[11] And this, as we have seen, was the substantial assumption of the Platonic Parmenides in his second retort.

It is clear therefore, that, when in *Parm.* 132 B *seq.* Plato puts into the mouth of the Eleate the two weighty principles enunciated above, he is adducing the actual tenets of the historical Parmenides as

---

[10] It matters little whether we follow Simplicius (*in Phys. A*, ed. Diels p. 87, 17) and translate "Thought is coincident with thought's object," or adopt Mr. Burnet's version (*Early Gr. Philos.* p. 186): "It is the same thing that can be thought and for the sake of which the thought exists." In the former case we identify the subject with the object of νόησις, in the the latter the object with the subject. Whichever rendering we choose, the argument will be the same, *viz.* $x = z$, and $y = z$, therefore $x = y$.

[11] I do not mean to imply that Parmenides himself expressly drew this inference, or spoke of τὸ ὄν as a νοῦς. We have no better authority for such an assertion than Plotinus *Enn.* v. 1. 8, and Simplicius *in Phys. A.* ed. Diels p. 143, 18 ff. Moreover, there is the negative evidence of Plato, who, in *Soph* 244 B, C, states that the Eleatics called their principle by the two names ἕν and ὄν, but makes no mention of νοῦς as a recognised appellation. My point is merely that the historical Parmenides' identification of νοούμενον and νοοῦν paved the way for the Platonic Parmenides' postulate of νοήματα νοοῦντα.

corrective of his own unrevised Idealism. And we begin to appreciate the dramatic propriety which caused him, at the expense of an obvious anachronism, to choose Parmenides as his critic.

But the full significance of that choice has not yet been sounded. If Parmenides held that the object thought was also the subject thinking, he did so only because he identified both alike with τὸ ὄν. And similarly Plato, who assumes that every νόημα νοεῖ, must base his assumption on the belief that in any process of νόησις the subject and the object are alike referable to a single underlying entity. That entity is described by him elsewhere in terms which correspond to the active and passive functions of the Ideal Minds. As they are νοήματα, so It is a νοητόν:

Tim. 37 A ψυχή, τῶν νοητῶν ἀεί τε ὄντων ὑπὸ τοῦ ἀρίστου ἀρίστη γενομένη τῶν γεννηθέντων.

As they are νοοῦντα, so It is a νοῦς:

Phileb. 30 C ἔστιν, ἃ πολλάκις εἰρήκαμεν, ἄπειρόν τε ἐν τῷ παντὶ πολὺ καὶ πέρας ἱκανὸν καί τις ἐπ' αὐτοῖς αἰτία οὐ φαύλη κοσμοῦσά τε καὶ συντάττουσα . . . σοφία καὶ νοῦς λεγομένη δικαιότατ' ἄν.

Laws 897 C ἡ ξύμπασα οὐρανοῦ ὁδὸς ἅμα καὶ φορὰ καὶ τῶν ἐν αὐτῷ ὄντων ἁπάντων νοῦ κινήσει καὶ περιφορᾷ καὶ λογισμοῖς ὁμοίαν φύσιν ἔχει.

This conception of a νοητὸς νοῦς and of νοήματα νοοῦντα may well have been the source of Aristotle's statements concerning τὰ ἄνευ ὕλης νοητά:

Met. Λ. 7. 1072 b 20 ἑαυτὸν δὲ νοεῖ ὁ νοῦς κατὰ μετάληψιν τοῦ νοητοῦ· νοητὸς γὰρ γίγνεται θιγγάνων καὶ νοῶν, ὥστε ταὐτὸν νοῦς καὶ νοητόν.

Ibid. Λ. 9. 1075 a 3 οὐχ ἑτέρου οὖν ὄντος τοῦ νοουμένου καὶ τοῦ νοῦ, ὅσα μὴ ὕλην ἔχει, τὸ αὐτὸ ἔσται καὶ ἡ νόησις τῷ νοουμένῳ μία.

Psych. Γ. 4. 12. 430 a 2 ὅπερ συμβαίνει ἐπὶ τοῦ νοῦ. καὶ αὐτὸς δὲ νοητός ἐστιν ὥσπερ τὰ νοητά. ἐπὶ μὲν γὰρ τῶν ἄνευ ὕλης τὸ αὐτό ἐστι τὸ νοοῦν καὶ τὸ νοούμενον.

Porph. *in Categ*. ed. Busse p. 91, 14 λέγω ὅτι αἰτιῶμαι αὐτὸν (Aristotle) ὅτι κυριώτατα κατὰ αὐτὸν καὶ μάλιστα καί πρώτως λεγομένων πρώτων οὐσιῶν τῶν νοητῶν οἷον τοῦ νοητοῦ θεοῦ καὶ τοῦ νοῦ καί, εἴπερ εἰσὶν ἰδέαι, καὶ τῶν ἰδεῶν, παριστὰς ταύτας πρώτας οὐσίας ἔφη τὰς ἐν τοῖς αἰσθητοῖς ἀτόμους.

But, be that as it may, unlooked for results have been reached. When Sokrates threw out his suggestion that the Idea might be a νόημα, he probably meant no more than a human thought or concept. By the aid of Parmenides' questions we have now come to see that the Ideas are beyond the reach of particular cognition:

Parm. 134 B Οὐκ ἄρα ὑπό γε ἡμῶν γιγνώσκεται τῶν εἰδῶν οὐδέν, ἐπειδὴ αὐτῆς ἐπιστήμης οὐ μετέχομεν.

We must in fact conceive them to be a plurality

of Minds into which one supreme Mind has multiplied itself, reproducing in them its own essential features of thinking and being thought. Hence, if they are called *νοήματα*, it is *primarily* because they are the thoughts of that Intelligence which is their underlying cause:

> Plut. *de placit. phil.* i. 10 Πλάτων χωριστὰς τῆς ὕλης οὐσίας τὰς ἰδέας ὑπολαμβάνει ἐν τοῖς νοήμασι καὶ ἐν ταῖς φαντασίαις τοῦ θεοῦ, τουτέστι τοῦ νοῦ, ὑφεστώσας.
>
> Stob. *Ecl.* I. x. 16a (Aetios), ed. Wachsmuth i. p. 127, 19 Πλάτων Ἀρίστωνος . . . ἰδέα δὲ οὐσία ἀσώματος ἐν τοῖς νοήμασι καὶ ταῖς φαντασίαις τοῦ θεοῦ.
>
> Proklos *in Parm.* ed. Cousin v. 148 συνέζευκται ἄρα ἀλλήλοις ὅ τε νοῦς καὶ τὰ εἴδη· καὶ εἰς τὴν συγγένειαν ταύτην, ὡς ἐμοὶ δοκεῖ, ἀποβλέπων καὶ ὁ Σωκράτης τὰ εἴδη νοήματα ἀφωρίσατο.—

secondarily because they mentally regard themselves and one another.

A scrutiny of *Parm.* 132 B *seq.* has brought us, then, to the following conclusion. Plato, at the time when he reconstituted his early theory of Ideas, held on the one hand that the object of any process of pure thought must be a single real existence, and on the other that such an object must itself possess the power of pure thinking. These two articles of belief he had adopted from the writings of Parmenides, a philosopher for whom he entertained the deepest reverence.¹² And further, he had adopted them on the original ground of their validity, namely the recognition of one underlying entity:

Parm. 128 A Μανθάνω, εἰπεῖν τὸν Σωκράτη, ὦ Παρμενίδη, . . . σὺ μὲν γὰρ ἐν τοῖς ποιήμασιν ἓν φῂς εἶναι τὸ πᾶν, καὶ τούτων τεκμήρια παρέχει καλῶς τε καὶ εὖ.

As applied to his own Idealism, their immediate result was to warrant him in positing *a single really existent Mind as basis and conditioning cause of a series of really existent Minds called the Ideas,*—the object of thought for any given Mind being itself or any other Mind. The relation thus formulated may be denoted, at any rate provisionally, by the accompanying diagram :—

νοητὸς νοῦς = The Supreme Mind.

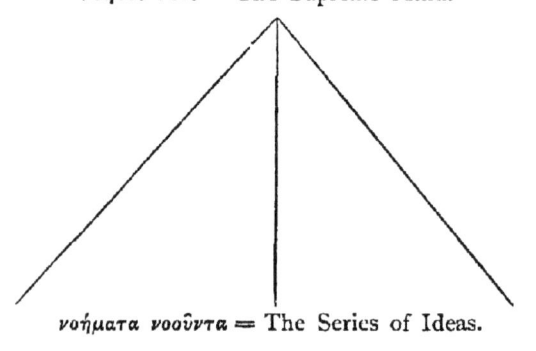

νοήματα νοοῦντα = The Series of Ideas.

---

¹² Cp. *Theaet.* 183 E Παρμενίδης δέ μοι φαίνεται, τὸ τοῦ Ὁμήρου, αἰδοῖός τέ μοι εἶναι ἅμα δεινός τε . . . καί μοι ἐφάνη βάθος τι ἔχειν παντάπασι γενναῖον, *Soph.* 237 A τὸν τοῦ πατρὸς Παρμενίδου λόγον.

§ II. *The Sophist.*

Thus far the components of the Platonic scheme have been characterised as ὄντα and as νοοῦντα—νοούμενα. It may now be shown that these characteristics involve certain further properties, without which any account of real and phenomenal nature would be altogether inadequate.

In *Soph.* 248 A the εἰδῶν φίλοι draw a distinction between γένεσις and οὐσία: the changeable nature of the former we apprehend through our body by means of sense-perception; the changeless nature of the latter we apprehend through our soul by means of reasoning. Again, in 248 C these same adherents of νοητὰ καὶ ἀσώματα εἴδη declare that γένεσις lies within, true οὐσία without, the domain of ποιεῖν καὶ πάσχειν.

While passing these opinions in review, the Eleate's remarks are supplementary rather than destructive. He points out that, if the Idealists hold, on the one hand that οὐσία γιγνώσκεται, and on the other hand that οὐσία is ἀπαθής, then—to avoid inconsistency—they must by the process which they describe as τὸ γιγνώσκειν ἢ τὸ γιγνώσκεσθαι mean something totally different from a ποίημα ἢ πάθος. If, however, τὸ γιγνώσκειν is in point of fact ποιεῖν τι—and the Stranger's words hint that such is the case—then they will allow that its correlative τὸ γιγνώσκεσθαι must be πάσχειν τι, and, still holding to their doctrine that οὐσία is γιγνωσκομένη ὑπὸ τῆς γνώσεως, they will admit that καθ' ὅσον γιγνώσκεται, κατὰ τοσοῦτον κινεῖται διὰ τὸ πάσχειν.

In this paragraph the Eleate's critique of Idealism brings before us two conceptions:

(i) That οὐσία is ἀπαθής, and—if truly known—must be known in some sense of the word "knowledge" which transcends the ποίημα ἢ πάθος properly attached to any process of γιγνώσκειν ἢ γιγνώσκεσθαι. What this higher intellectual state may be we are not yet told, but bearing in mind the ὄντα of the Parmenides, which were further determined as νοοῦντα and νοούμενα, we shall presume that it is νόησις, pure thought, and our presumption will be justified by the immediate sequel.

(ii) That οὐσία πάσχει,—so far at least as it provides an object for γνῶσις, rightly so called,—and that therein it departs from its own ἠρεμία.

In effect the Stranger rules, and Theaetetus accepts his ruling, that οὐσία is double-faced:

(i) As the subject and object of νόησις it is ἀπαθής.[13]

(ii) As the subject and object of γνῶσις it πάσχει.

---

[13] Arist. *Topica* Z. 10. 148 a 20 ἀπαθεῖς γὰρ καὶ ἀκίνητοι δοκοῦσιν αἱ ἰδέαι τοῖς λέγουσιν ἰδέας εἶναι, *frag.* 184. 1510 a 4 ἔτι διαιρεταὶ ἂν εἶεν αἱ ἰδέαι καὶ μεριστοί, οὖσαι ἀπαθεῖς, Diog. Laert. III. 12, 13 ἔστι δὲ τῶν εἰδῶν ἐν ἕκαστον ἀΐδιόν τε καὶ νόημα καὶ πρὸς τούτοις ἀπαθές. Hence Ideal monads are said to be ἀπαθεῖς in *Met.* A. 9. 991 b 26 οὐδὲν γὰρ αὐταῖς οἷόν τε ὑπάρχειν πάθος, *ibid.* M. 8. 1083 a 9. Compare Aristotle's

Can we, however, reconcile these opposing conceptions? Can we predicate both aspects alike of the same οὐσία? This is the problem to which the Eleate now addresses himself in a passage of unusual lucidity and directness.

He contends (249 A) that τὸ παντελῶς ὂν cannot be σεμνὸν καὶ ἅγιον, νοῦν οὐκ ἔχον. And if νοῦς be present, we shall be forced, he says, to admit also ζωή, ψυχή, and κίνησις. At the same time we must be careful to retain that element of στάσις, without which νοῦς could not anywhere exist.

Οὐσία then, wherever it is found, will be endowed with two qualities which are ἐναντιώτατα ἀλλήλοις, namely:—

(i) with στάσις, in which case we have νοῦς;

(ii) with κίνησις, in which case we have ζωὴ and ψυχή.

Soph. 249 D τῷ δὴ φιλοσόφῳ ... πᾶσα ἀνάγκη ... κατὰ τὴν τῶν παίδων εὐχὴν ὅσα ἀκίνητα καὶ κεκινημένα τὸ ὄν τε καὶ τὸ πᾶν ξυναμφότερα[14] λέγειν.

---

own doctrine: *Psych. A.* 4. 14. 408 *b* 29 ὁ δὲ νοῦς ἴσως θειότερόν τι καὶ ἀπαθές ἐστιν, *ibid.* Γ. 5. 1. 430 *a* 17 καὶ οὗτος ὁ νοῦς (the νοῦς ποιητικός) χωριστὸς καὶ ἀμιγὴς καὶ ἀπαθής, τῇ οὐσίᾳ ὢν ἐνεργείᾳ, *Met. Λ.* 7. 1073 *a* 11 which predicates ἀπαθὲς καὶ ἀναλλοίωτον of the οὐσία ... ἀΐδιος καὶ ἀκίνητος καὶ κεχωρισμένη τῶν αἰσθητῶν. Hermes (quoted by Stob. *Ecl.* I. lxi. 1, ed. Wachsmuth i. p. 275, 17) has ὁ νοῦς ἀπαθής.

[14] This explains why the definition of ὄντως ὂν given in *Soph.* 247 E, 248 C was regarded as provisional and not final. "Whatever possesses

Applying this all-important result to the issues of last section, we note that the argument from the *Parmenides* dealt with only one side of the truth. It regarded οὐσία as the subject and object of νόησις, without taking into account any lower intellectual faculty, such as that of γνῶσις or λογισμός. The *Sophist* warns us against persisting in such neglect. It bids us to observe that the supreme νοῦς of the *Philebus* is not only a νοῦς, but also a νοητὸν ζῷον—

Cp. *Tim.* 39 E ἵνα τόδ᾽ ὡς ὁμοιότατον ᾖ τῷ τελέῳ καὶ νοητῷ ζῴῳ πρὸς τὴν τῆς διαιωνίας μίμησιν φύσεως.

Phileb. 30 D Οὐκοῦν ἐν . . . τῇ τοῦ Διὸς ἐρεῖς φύσει βασιλικὴν μὲν ψυχήν, βασιλικὸν δὲ νοῦν ἐγγίγνεσθαι διὰ τὴν τῆς αἰτίας δύναμιν—

and that the ideal νοήματα of the *Parmenides* are not only νοήματα, but also νοητὰ ζῷα—

Cp. *Tim.* 30 C τὰ γὰρ δὴ νοητὰ ζῷα πάντα ἐκεῖνο ἐν ἑαυτῷ περιλαβὸν ἔχει.

Ibid. 31 A τὸ γὰρ περιέχον πάντα, ὁπόσα νοητὰ ζῷα.—

inasmuch as every νοῦς, whether supreme or sub-

---

the power of doing or suffering" would indeed aptly characterise οὐσία *quâ* subject and object of γνῶσις. But *quâ* subject and object of νόησις this same οὐσία was admitted to be ἀπαθής. Consequently, unless δύναμις can be taken to denote the power of passing from the first or static into the second or kinetic condition, we must substitute the amended definition implied in 249 D.

$$\overbrace{\qquad\qquad\qquad\qquad\qquad\qquad}^{\tau\grave{o}\ \pi\hat{a}\nu}$$

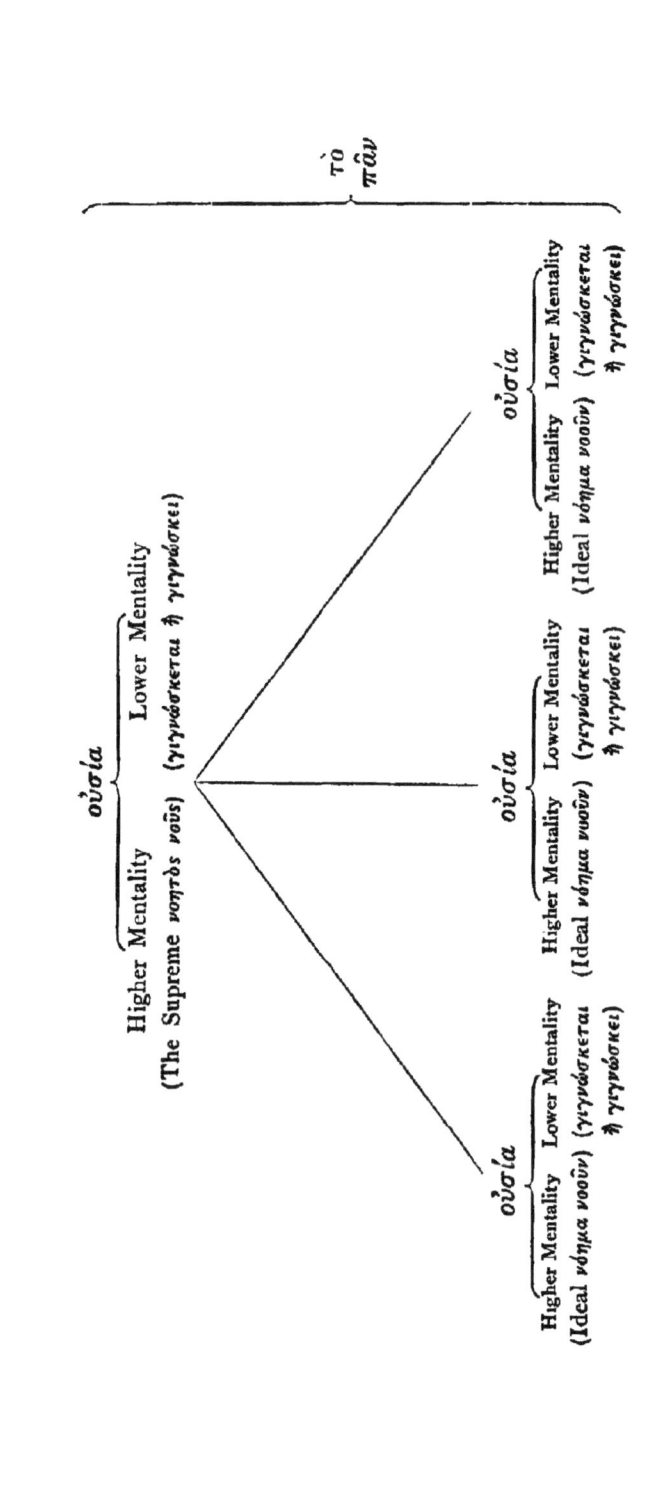

$$\underbrace{\overbrace{\text{Higher Mentality}}\ \overbrace{\text{Lower Mentality}}}_{\text{ο}\dot{\text{υ}}\text{σία}}$$
(The Supreme νοητὸς νοῦς) (γιγνώσκεται ἢ γιγνώσκει)

$$\underbrace{\overbrace{\text{Higher Mentality}}\ \overbrace{\text{Lower Mentality}}}_{\text{ο}\dot{\text{υ}}\text{σία}}$$
(Ideal νόημα νοοῦν) (γιγνώσκεται ἢ γιγνώσκει)

$$\underbrace{\overbrace{\text{Higher Mentality}}\ \overbrace{\text{Lower Mentality}}}_{\text{ο}\dot{\text{υ}}\text{σία}}$$
(Ideal νόημα νοοῦν) (γιγνώσκεται ἢ γιγνώσκει)

$$\underbrace{\overbrace{\text{Higher Mentality}}\ \overbrace{\text{Lower Mentality}}}_{\text{ο}\dot{\text{υ}}\text{σία}}$$
(Ideal νόημα νοοῦν) (γιγνώσκεται ἢ γιγνώσκει)

ordinate, is forced by the necessary nature of its own οὐσία to pass out of its tranquil ἀπάθεια into the ποιήματα and παθήματα of animation.[15] Thus by emphasising the fact that, *wherever*[16] pure thought is found, there will its shadow the lower mental phase be found also, it enables us to extend our previous scheme as in the diagram.

§ III. *Aristotle's Psychology.*

Having learnt in the preceding section that all οὐσία deserving of the name must necessarily pass from higher to lower phase, we have yet to enquire

---

[15] For Plato's conviction that νοῦς must be attached to ψυχή see the following passages: *Phileb.* 30 C σοφία μὴν καὶ νοῦς ἄνευ ψυχῆς οὐκ ἄν ποτε γενοίσθην, *Parm.* 132 B μὴ τῶν εἰδῶν ἕκαστον ᾖ τούτων νόημα, καὶ οὐδαμοῦ αὐτῷ προσήκῃ ἐγγίγνεσθαι ἄλλοθι ἢ ἐν ψυχαῖς, *Soph.* 249 A ἀλλὰ ταῦτα μὲν ἀμφότερα (νοῦς and ζωή) ἐνόντ' αὐτῷ λέγομεν, οὐ μὴν ἐν ψυχῇ γε φήσομεν αὐτὸ ἔχειν αὐτά, καὶ τίν' ἂν ἕτερον ἔχοι τρόπον, *Tim.* 30 B νοῦν δ' αὖ χωρὶς ψυχῆς ἀδύνατον παραγενέσθαι τῳ, *Ibid.* 46 D τῶν γὰρ ὄντων ᾧ νοῦν μόνῳ κτᾶσθαι προσήκει, λεκτέον ψυχήν. Compare Arist. *Psych.* Γ. 4. 429a 27 καὶ εὖ δὴ οἱ λέγοντες τὴν ψυχὴν εἶναι τόπον εἰδῶν, πλὴν ὅτι οὔτε ὅλη ἀλλ' ἡ νοητική, οὔτε ἐντελεχείᾳ ἀλλὰ δυνάμει τὰ εἴδη, *Met* Λ. 3. 1070a 26 ἡ ψυχὴ . . . μὴ πᾶσα ἀλλ' ὁ νοῦς, Archytas in *frag. phil. Gr.* ed. Mullach 1, 565 αἴσθασις μὲν ἐν σώματι γίνεται, νόος δ' ἐν ψυχᾷ.

[16] See *Soph.* 249 B ξυμβαίνει δ' οὖν, ὦ Θεαίτητε, ἀκινήτων τε ὄντων νοῦν μηδενὶ περὶ μηδενὸς εἶναι μηδαμοῦ, the counterpart of 249 C Τί δ', ἄνευ τούτων (sc. τοῦ κατὰ ταὐτὰ κ.τ.λ.) νοῦν καθορᾷς ὄντα ἢ γενόμενον ἂν καὶ ὁπουοῦν; Ἥκιστα.

how this passage may be effected, transporting us as it does from the realm of serene intelligence—

Tim. 52 A τὸ κατὰ ταὐτὰ εἶδος ἔχον, ἀγένητον καὶ ἀνώλεθρον, οὔτε εἰς ἑαυτὸ εἰσδεχόμενον ἄλλο ἄλλοθεν οὔτε αὐτὸ εἰς ἄλλο ποι ἰόν, ἀόρατον δὲ καὶ ἄλλως ἀναίσθητον, τοῦτο ὃ δὴ νόησις εἴληχεν ἐπισκοπεῖν—

to the world of complex sensitivity—

Laws 896 E ἄγει μὲν δὴ ψυχὴ πάντα τὰ κατ᾽ οὐρανὸν καὶ γῆν καὶ θάλατταν ταῖς αὑτῆς κινήσεσιν, αἷς ὀνόματά ἐστι βούλεσθαι, σκοπεῖσθαι, ἐπιμελεῖσθαι, βουλεύεσθαι, δοξάζειν ὀρθῶς, ἐψευσμένως, χαίρουσαν, λυπουμένην, θαρροῦσαν, φοβουμένην, μισοῦσαν, στέργουσαν, καὶ πάσαις ὅσαι τούτων ξυγγενεῖς ἢ πρωτουργοὶ κινήσεις τὰς δευτερουργοὺς αὖ παραλαμβάνουσαι κινήσεις σωμάτων ἄγουσι πάντα εἰς αὔξησιν καὶ φθίσιν καὶ διάκρισιν καὶ σύγκρισιν.

The method of transition will, I think, be best followed by the aid of a vexed paragraph in Aristotle's *Psychology*. I shall first state what I take to be the argument of that paragraph; and then offer some justification for the meaning which I assign to its several parts.

Aristotle's thesis is (*Psych.* A. 2. 6. 404*b* 8) that those thinkers, who find the main characteristic of ψυχὴ in τὸ γινώσκειν καὶ τὸ αἰσθάνεσθαι, identify ψυχὴ with their ἀρχὴ or ἀρχαί. Empedokles, for example, constructs the percipient soul out of the same six elements which go to form the percepts of his system. And that Plato acted in a similar way may be inferred from three considerations[17] :—

(i) In the *Timaeus* Plato makes both ἡ ψυχὴ and τὰ πράγματα out of the same elements (*sc.* ταὐτὸν and θάτερον, combining to produce οὐσία).

(ii) In τὰ περὶ φιλοσοφίας λεγόμενα he distinguishes four stages in the evolution of the percipient Idea corresponding to four stages in the evolution of the percept Ideas. These four are ἡ τοῦ ἑνὸς ἰδέα, and πρῶτον μῆκος, πρῶτον πλάτος, πρῶτον βάθος.

(iii) The percipient Idea thus evolved apprehends by means of four faculties (namely νοῦς, and ἐπιστήμη, δόξα, αἴσθησις), which correlate with four εἴδη τῶν πραγμάτων, *i.e.* with things grouped according to the said four stages in the evolution of the percept Ideas.

For these reasons Aristotle concludes that Plato, like Empedokles, constructed the subject and the

---

[17] I append the exact words: *Psych.* A. 2. 7. 404b 16 τὸν αὐτὸν δὲ τρόπον καὶ Πλάτων ἐν τῷ Τιμαίῳ τὴν ψυχὴν ἐκ τῶν στοιχείων ποιεῖ· γινώσκεσθαι γὰρ τῷ ὁμοίῳ τ᾽ ὅμοιον, τὰ δὲ πράγματα ἐκ τῶν ἀρχῶν εἶναι. ὁμοίως δὲ καὶ ἐν τοῖς περὶ φιλοσοφίας λεγομένοις διωρίσθη, αὐτὸ μὲν τὸ ζῷον ἐξ αὐτῆς τῆς τοῦ ἑνὸς ἰδέας καὶ τοῦ πρώτου μήκους καὶ πλάτους καὶ βάθους, τὰ δ᾽ ἄλλα ὁμοιοτρόπως. ἔτι δὲ καὶ ἄλλως, νοῦν μὲν τὸ ἕν, ἐπιστήμην δὲ τὰ δύο—μοναχῶς γὰρ ἐφ᾽ ἕν—,τὸν δὲ τοῦ ἐπιπέδου ἀριθμὸν δόξαν, αἴσθησιν δὲ τὸν τοῦ στερεοῦ· οἱ μὲν γὰρ ἀριθμοὶ τὰ εἴδη αὐτὰ καὶ ἀρχαὶ ἐλέγοντο—εἰσὶ δ᾽ ἐκ τῶν στοιχείων—,κρίνεται δὲ τὰ πράγματα τὰ μὲν νῷ, τὰ δ᾽ ἐπιστήμῃ, τὰ δὲ δόξῃ, τὰ δ᾽ αἰσθήσει· εἴδη δ᾽ οἱ ἀριθμοὶ οὗτοι τῶν πραγμάτων.

object of cognition out of the same constituents and by parallel processes, thereby preserving the law γινώσκεσθαι τὸ ὅμοιον τῷ ὁμοίῳ (*Psych.* A. 2. 20. 405 b 15).

i. The first of the three clauses here summarised represents Plato as arguing to this effect:—

(*a*) Like is known by like.

(*b*) τὰ πράγματα (*i.e.* things in general, the *object* of knowledge) are formed ἐκ τῶν ἀρχῶν.

(*c*) Therefore ψυχή too (the *subject*[18] of knowledge) must be made ἐκ τῶν στοιχείων.

This conclusion, says Aristotle, is to be found in the *Timaeus*. And we can hardly doubt that he refers on the one hand to *Tim.* 35 A, where the cosmic soul is composed of ταὐτόν and θάτερον, which coalesce to produce οὐσία; and on the other hand to *Tim.* 41 D, where the subordinate souls are compounded of the same ingredients, though in a less pure condition. It seems certain, therefore, that by τὰ στοιχεῖα Aristotle here denotes the principles of Identity and of Difference, which are represented in the *Timaeus* by the symbols ταὐτόν and θάτερον.

Again, the force of the argument depends on the identification of these στοιχεῖα with αἱ ἀρχαί. It has, indeed, been suggested that τὰ στοιχεῖα are ταὐτόν, θάτερον and οὐσία considered as the elements of the

---

[18] Cp. Simplic. *in Arist. Psych.* ed. Hayduck p. 29, 11 ἀνῆγον τοίνυν εἰς τὰς ἀρχὰς τά τε γνωστὰ πάντα, τουτέστι τὰ ὄντα, καὶ τὰς γνωστικὰς τούτων δυνάμεις.

material world, whereas αἱ ἀρχαί are the same principles considered as the constituents of the immaterial soul; but I fail to find adequate support for such a view in either Platonic or Aristotelian diction. If any distinction is to be drawn,[19] I should prefer to say that ταὐτὸν and θάτερον regarded by themselves as ultimate principles are ἀρχαί, regarded as the elements of derived existences are στοιχεῖα: cp.

Arist. *Met.* N. 4. 1091*b* 3 διὰ τὸ τὸ ἓν ἀρχὴν καὶ ἀρχὴν ὡς στοιχεῖον καὶ τὸν ἀριθμὸν ἐκ τοῦ ἑνός.

Ibid. N. 4. 1091*b* 19 τὸ μὲν φάναι τὴν ἀρχὴν τοιαύτην εἶναι εὔλογον ἀληθὲς εἶναι· τὸ μέντοι ταύτην εἶναι τὸ ἕν, ἢ εἰ μὴ τοῦτο, στοιχεῖόν τε καὶ στοιχεῖον ἀριθμῶν, ἀδύνατον.

Ibid. N. 4. 1092*a* 6 ἀρχὴν πᾶσαν στοιχεῖον ποιοῦσι.

However that may be, both terms are regularly employed by Aristotle to describe the same two bases of Platonism: *e.g.*

Met. N. 1. 1087*b* 12 ἀλλὰ μὴν καὶ τὰς ἀρχὰς ἃς στοιχεῖα καλοῦσιν οὐ καλῶς ἀποδιδόασιν οἱ ... τὸ μέγα καὶ τὸ μικρὸν λέγοντες μετὰ τοῦ ἑνὸς τρία ταῦτα στοιχεῖα τῶν ἀριθμῶν.

Ibid M. 9. 1086*a* 26 ἐπεὶ οὖν λέγουσί τινες τοιαύτας εἶναι τὰς ἰδέας καὶ τοὺς ἀριθμούς, καὶ τὰ τούτων στοιχεῖα τῶν ὄντων εἶναι στοιχεῖα καὶ ἀρχάς, σκεπτέον κ.τ.λ.

---

[19] Stob. *Ecl.* I. x. 16*b*, ed. Wachsmuth i. p. 128, 14 has οἱ μὲν οὖν περὶ Ἀριστοτέλην καὶ Πλάτωνα διαφέρειν ἡγοῦνται ἀρχὴν καὶ στοιχεῖα.

And if the substitution of τῶν ἀρχῶν for τῶν στοιχείων within the bounds of a single argument seem strange, it is corroborated by the similar case of

Met. M. 7. 1081 b 31 ἀνάγκη δ', ἐπείπερ ἔσται τὸ ἓν καὶ ἡ ἀόριστος δυὰς στοιχεῖα. εἰ δ' ἀδύνατα τὰ συμβαίνοντα, καὶ τὰς ἀρχὰς εἶναι ταύτας ἀδύνατον.

The outcome of this first clause, therefore, is that ψυχή—which is an οὐσία inasmuch as it is composed of ταὐτὸν and θάτερον—has for the content of its cognitions objects formed of the same constituents as itself, in short other psychic οὐσίαι. And whereas, when dealing with νόησις only, we concluded that the object of thought for any given Mind is itself or any other Mind, we have now extended the same conclusion to the whole ψυχὴ whereof νοῦς is the static phase, and are prepared to affirm that the object of cognition for any such ἔμψυχον is itself or any similar ἔμψυχον.

Moreover in the terms ταὐτὸν and θάτερον we have obtained a convenient notation[20] for higher and lower psychosis, which permits us to re-edit our scheme in the appended form.

ii. The precise import of the second clause is less

---

[20] Foreshadowed in dialogues earlier than the *Timaeus*, *e.g.* *Soph.* 249 B τὸ κατὰ ταὐτὰ καὶ ὡσαύτως καὶ περὶ τὸ αὐτό κ.τ.λ. *Parm.* 158 C τὴν ἑτέραν φύσιν τοῦ εἴδους (= *Tim.* 35 A τὴν θατέρου φύσιν).

$$\overbrace{\qquad\qquad\qquad\qquad\qquad\qquad\qquad\qquad\qquad}^{\tau\grave{o}\ \pi\hat{a}\nu}$$

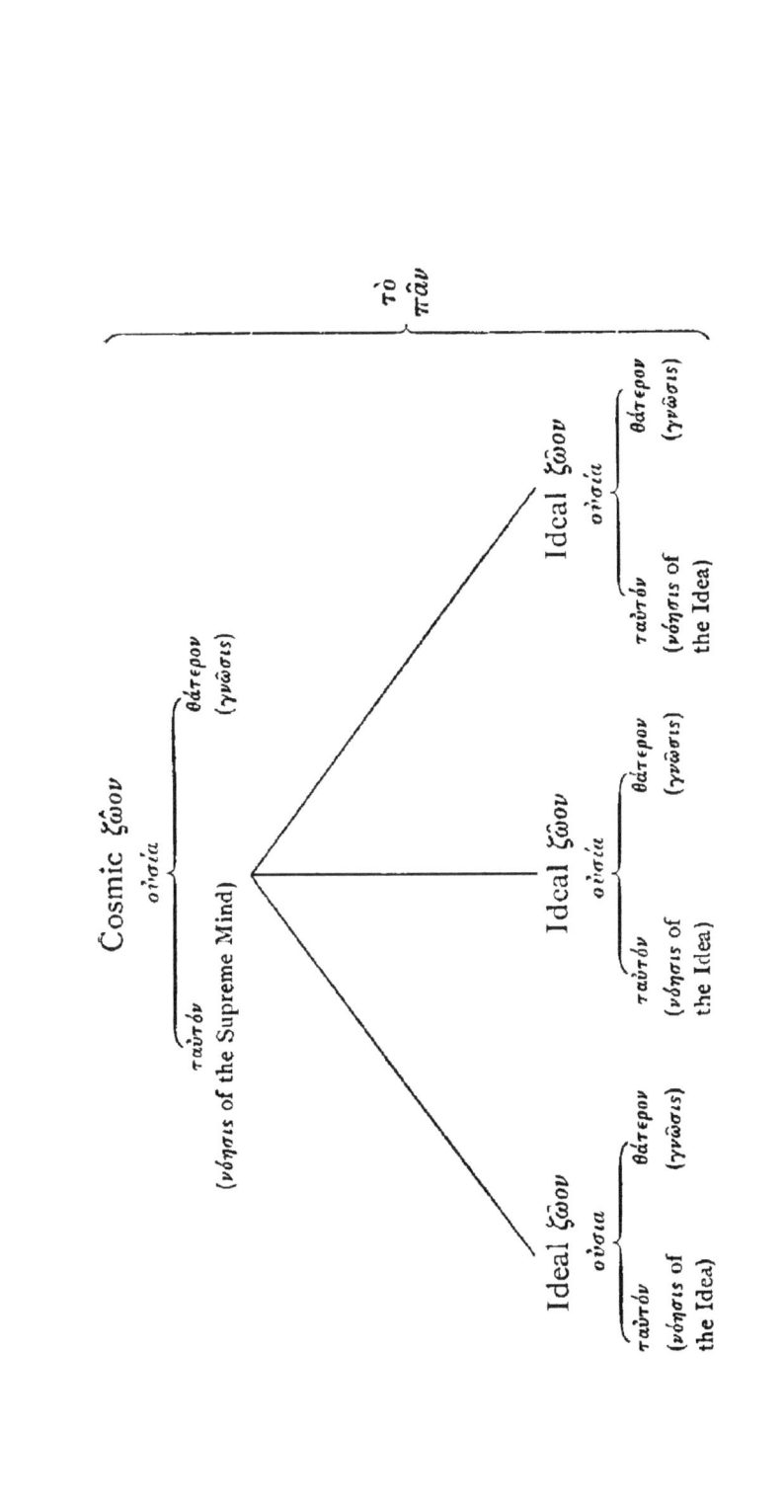

Cosmic ζῷον
$\underbrace{\qquad\qquad}_{\text{οὐσία}}$
$\overbrace{\ }^{\theta\acute{a}\tau\epsilon\rho o\nu}$ (γνῶσις)
$\underbrace{\ }_{\tau\alpha\grave{v}\tau\acute{o}\nu}$ (νόησις of the Supreme Mind)

Ideal ζῷον — οὐσία
 — ταὐτόν (νόησις of the Idea)
 — θάτερον (γνῶσις)

Ideal ζῷον — οὐσία
 — ταὐτόν (νόησις of the Idea)
 — θάτερον (γνῶσις)

Ideal ζῷον — οὐσία
 — ταὐτόν (νόησις of the Idea)
 — θάτερον (γνῶσις)

easy to determine; and widely divergent views have been advanced, of which some account must be rendered before further progress is possible.

Simplicius (*in Arist. Psych* ed. Hayduck p. 28, 22 *seqq*) takes the whole clause ὁμοίως δὲ καὶ ... τὰ δ' ἄλλα ὁμοιοτρόπως to be descriptive of τὰ γνωστά, the objects known: the next words, ἔτι δὲ καὶ ἄλλως .... αἴσθησιν δὲ τὸν τοῦ στερεοῦ, then denote τὰ γνωστικά, the subjects knowing: and the concluding lines, οἱ μὲν γὰρ ἀριθμοὶ ... οἱ ἀριθμοὶ οὗτοι τῶν πραγμάτων, point the parallelism between object and subject. But, apart from the fact that (*a*) the words ἔτι δὲ καὶ ἄλλως clearly mark a third exposition coordinate with τὸν αὐτὸν δὲ τρόπον κ.τ.λ. and ὁμοίως δὲ καὶ κ.τ.λ. rather than a mere sub-section, this division (*b*) introduces special difficulties into the passage with which we are immediately concerned. For, granted that by αὐτὸ τὸ ζῷον is meant the intelligible world[21] (ὁ νοητὸς διάκοσμος ἐν ᾧ τὰ αὐτοειδῆ), and by τὰ ἄλλα the knowable opinable and sensible world (τὰ λοιπὰ τῆς τῶν γνωστῶν διαιρέσεως

---

[21] I fail to see any such justification for the term as Mr. Wallace (ed. Arist. *Psych.* p. 205) finds in *Tim.* 30 B οὕτως οὖν δὴ κατὰ λόγον τὸν εἰκότα δεῖ λέγειν τόνδε τὸν κόσμον ζῷον ἔμψυχον ἔννουν τε τῇ ἀληθείᾳ διὰ τοῦ θεοῦ γενέσθαι πρόνοιαν. The cosmos can only be described as a ζῷον in so far as its intelligibility implies the evolution of ἐπιστητά, δοξαστά, αἰσθητά—and this is just what Simplicius would exclude; for these he finds in τὰ ἄλλα.

τὰ ἐπιστητὰ τὰ δοξαστὰ τὰ αἰσθητά), it can hardly be said that the latter is constructed ὁμοιοτρόπως with regard to the former. Simplicius himself acknowledges τὰ ἄλλα to be ἐκ τῶν ἀρχῶν μὲν ... τῶν εἰδῶν, ἀλλ' οὐκέτι ἐκ τῶν αὐτοαρχῶν ὡς ἐκ στοιχείων, ἀλλ' ἐξ ἐκείνων μέν, ὡς ἐξῃρημένων < δὲ > αἰτίων τῶν ἑκάστοις συστοίχων.

Themistius, who (66 B, ed. Spengel p. 20 *seqq.*) similarly finds in the words ὁμοίως δὲ καὶ ... ὁμοιοτρόπως a description of the cosmos as object thought, and in the succeeding clause an account of the soul as subject thinking, is liable to the same objections, *viz.* (*a*) that in the words ὁμοίως δὲ καὶ ... ὁμοιοτρόπως we expect to discover a comparison between γνωστικὸν and γνωστόν, not between different kinds of γνωστά, and (*b*) that the phrase τὰ δ' ἄλλα ὁμοιοτρόπως is an over-statement[22] of the case.

Nor does Philoponus (C. fol. 2 A) improve upon this by understanding τὰ ἄλλα of such ill-assorted elements as τὰ νοητά, τὰ φυσικά, and τὰ αἰσθητά. As Trendelenburg remarks—" Neo-Platonica satis olent."

Lastly, Sophonias gives, along with much irrelevant matter, the view of his predecessors (*de Anim. paraph.* ed. Hayduck p. 13, 6), making both members

---

[22] Themistius' explanation is τὸ μὲν οὖν αὐτοζῷον, τουτέστι τὸν κόσμον τὸν νοητόν, ἐκ τῶν πρώτων ἐποίουν ἀρχῶν, τὰ δὲ ἐπὶ μέρους ἐκ τῶν ὑφειμένων· ὥσπερ γὰρ τὰ αἰσθητὰ ἔχει πρὸς ἄλληλα, οὕτω καὶ τὰς ἰδέας αὐτῶν πρὸς ἀλλήλας ἔχειν (ed. Spengel p. 21).

of the clause under discussion descriptive of the object of cognition: τέτταρα γὰρ αὐτῷ ... στοιχεῖα ... τοῦ νοητοῦ διακόσμου πεποίηνται, ἐν ᾧ τὸ τῶν ἰδεῶν πλήρωμα· τὸ αὐτοέν, ἡ αὐτοδυάς, ἡ αὐτοτριὰς καὶ ἡ αὐτοτετράς, ἀφ᾽ ὧνπερ καὶ ὁ αἰσθητὸς οὗτος κόσμος ἤρτηται ὡς ἀπ᾽ αἰτίου τοῦ νοητοῦ καὶ αἱ ἀρχαὶ αὐτοῦ ἐκεῖθεν.

Passing from the older commentators to more recent interpreters, we find Trendelenburg—though in several points correcting their extravagance—still misled by them as to the sequence of the main argument:

"Ita et Plato, quemadmodum pergitur, ut similia similibus cognoscerentur, eosdem numeros αὐτοζώου fecit, eosdem *menti* indidit. Sic utraque loci pars artissime coniungenda, neque altera ab altera divellenda, quasi ab illo ἔτι δὲ καὶ ἄλλως novi quid incipiatur."[23]

The result of this misconception is that he fails to explain the words τὰ δ᾽ ἄλλα ὁμοιοτρόπως:

"Quae fuerint haec reliqua, non definimus, universas tantum ideas, ne quid Platoni obtrudatur, intellegentes."[24]

He is aware that the explanations propounded by Simplicius and Philoponus are unsatisfactory, but has little to offer in their stead.

---

[23] Arist. *de anima*, ed. 1877, p. 187.
[24] *Ibid.* p. 188.

Others have seen that the key to the passage lies in the very "divulsio" which Trendelenburg deprecates. Dr. Jackson, for example, proposes to translate αὐτὸ τὸ ζῷον by "the universal *Subject*"[25] and τὰ ἄλλα by "the universal *Object*." This is a distinct move in the right direction: it is, however, open to criticism on the following grounds:—

(α) An inexact and therefore unsatisfactory meaning is attached to the words which describe "the universal Subject:"

αὐτὸ μὲν τὸ ζῷον ἐξ αὐτῆς τῆς τοῦ ἑνὸς ἰδέας καὶ τοῦ πρώτου μήκους καὶ πλάτους καὶ βάθους.

The phrase αὐτῆς τῆς τοῦ ἑνὸς ἰδέας would thus be loosely used for αὐτοῦ τοῦ ἑνός.

(β) Elsewhere in Aristotle the term αὐτὸ τὸ ζῷον signifies merely the Idea from which a particular animal derives its animality, the Idea of "animal," *e.g.* Met. Z. 14. 1039 b 9—16 πολλὰ ἔσται αὐτὸ τὸ ζῷον κ.τ.λ. *ibid.* M. 9. 1085 a 26 πότερον τὸ ζῷον αὐτὸ ἐν τῷ ζῴῳ ἢ ἕτερον αὐτοῦ ζῴου, *frag.* 184. 1510 a 14 ᾗ μὲν καὶ ζῷόν ἐστι, μετέχοι ἂν καὶ αὐτοῦ τοῦ ζῴου. Plato himself employs the plural of the same term to describe the Ideas of animals generally:

---

[25] That is, the supreme Νοῦς in its passage into cosmic existence, as opposed to that cosmic existence which originates from the evolution of the supreme Νοῦς.

Rep. 532 A πρὸς αὐτὰ ἤδη τὰ ζῷα ἐπιχειρεῖν ἀποβλέπειν καὶ πρὸς αὐτὰ ἄστρα κ.τ.λ.

I conclude, therefore, that to *restrict* the phrase to "the universal Subject" is a limitation unwarranted by either Aristotelian or Platonic usage.

Mr. Wallace, who interprets αὐτὸ τὸ ζῷον as "the subject knowing" *i.e.* the microcosm, and τὰ ἄλλα as "the objects known" *i.e.* the macrocosm, escapes the first of these objections—because the particular ζῷον (the microcosm) is of course the given Idea (ἡ τοῦ ἑνὸς ἰδέα) as it appears in three-dimensional space. But he too traverses the terminology of Aristotle, who by αὐτὸ τὸ ζῷον elsewhere denotes not a particular[26] but an Idea.

Another suggestion takes both αὐτὸ τὸ ζῷον and τὰ ἄλλα as "subjects"—the contrast between subject and object being not expressed but only implied in the sentence. The former will then mean the supreme ζῷον; the latter the subordinate ζῷα. This view, apart from its liability to the objections which I have brought against Dr. Jackson's version, seems to me to destroy the balance of Aristotle's triple argument. We should have him adducing three clauses for the express purpose of pointing out the similarity between subject

---

[26] Plato, according to Mr. Archer-Hind's rendering, uses αὐτὸ τὸ ζῷον of the individual animal in *Tim.* 89 B: but the passage, as we shall see, may be taken differently.

and object, and then omitting to make any mention of that object in the central clause of the three.[27]

It is, I think, possible to rectify all these flaws by understanding αὐτὸ τὸ ζῷον as "*the absolute animal*," that is *any given* νοητὸν ζῷον—(whether it be the παντελὲς ζῷον of *Tim.* 31 B, or one of the ἐν μέρους εἴδει ζῷα of *Tim.* 30 C),—and τὰ ἄλλα as "*the remaining absolute animals*." This somewhat obvious rendering of the words τὰ ἄλλα is suggested by Philoponus (C. 2 τὰ δ' ἄλλα ὁμοιοτρόπως, τὰ ἄλλα, ἤτοι . . . ἢ τὰ ἄλλα παραδείγματα, οἷον τὸ αὐτόκαλον, τὸ αὐτοάνθρωπος, καὶ ἐπὶ τῶν λοιπῶν ὁμοίως) and strongly supported by the variant readings τὰς δ' ἄλλας ὁμοιοτρόπους (Themist. 66 B) and τὰς ἄλλας ὁμοιοτρόπως (Philop. C. 2), which refer clearly to the remaining ἰδέαι. That the phrase is a natural one may be gathered from such expressions as the following :—

Tim. 30 C οὗ ἔστι τἆλλα ζῷα καθ' ἓν καὶ κατὰ γένη μόρια.

Ibid. 90 E τὰ γὰρ ἄλλα ζῷα ᾗ γέγονεν αὖ κ.τ.λ.

Phaedr. 247 E καὶ τἆλλα ὡσαύτως τὰ ὄντα ὄντως θεασαμένη κ.τ.λ.

---

[27] This is in a manner the converse of Trendelenburg's error. For he, following the lead of the Greek commentators, held that both parts of the clause referred to the *objects* of cognition; and the present suggestion makes both parts refer to the *subjects* of cognition.

Both the given ζῷον as percipient and the remaining ζῷα as percepts are constructed ὁμοιοτρόπως, since in every case an absolute animal if subjected to logical analysis will be found to consist of that form of τὸ ἕν which is appropriate to itself (hence the article τῆς τοῦ ἑνὸς ἰδέας) and the successive dimensions through which it is evolved.

This interpretation escapes the two objections urged on p. 34 by admitting the claim of any and every intelligible animal to the title αὐτὸ τὸ ζῷον, instead of confining the term to the supreme ζῷον.[28] It preserves too the symmetry of the argument; and that, not only by emphasising Aristotle's main contention—the similarity between percipient and percept—but also by identifying the subject of the present with that of the preceding sentence: for in the first clause we saw that any given ἔμψυχον—whether it be the whole cosmic ζῷον or one of the partial Ideal ζῷα—is formed out of the same elements as the other ἔμψυχα which constitute the objects of its cognition; and now in the second clause we see that any given αὐτὸ ζῷον —whether it be the whole cosmic animal or

---

[28] As a matter of fact—excluding *Tim.* 89 B, at present *sub judice*—the supreme ζῷον is not elsewhere, either in Plato or Aristotle, called αὐτὸ τὸ ζῷον. It is however spoken of as αὐτὸ ζῷον in *Tim.* 37 C, D ὡς δὲ κινηθὲν αὐτὸ καὶ ζῶν ἐνόησε ... καθάπερ οὖν αὐτὸ τυγχάνει ζῷον ἀΐδιον ὄν κ.τ.λ., which is perhaps the passage referred to by Proklos on *Tim.* 4 C ἡ νοητὴ πάντων αἰτία καὶ παραδειγματικὴ τῶν ὑπὸ τοῦ δημιουργοῦ ποιουμένων, ἣν καὶ αὐτοζῷον διὰ τοῦτο καλεῖν ὁ Πλάτων ἠξίωσεν.

one of the partial Ideal animals—is developed through the same four stages as the other ζῷα which constitute the objects of its cognition. The argument, I conceive, is exactly parallel in the first two clauses, and raises a presumption that it will be so in the third also.

But before passing to the last consideration we must enquire further concerning the nature of the four stages that have hitherto been mentioned without comment. Aristotle alludes to them again in *Met. M.* 2 1077 a 24 ἔτι αἱ γενέσεις δηλοῦσιν. πρῶτον μὲν γὰρ ἐπὶ μῆκος γίγνεται, εἶτα ἐπὶ πλάτος, τελευταῖον δ᾽ εἰς βάθος, καὶ τέλος ἔσχεν. And his remarks both there and here are best elucidated by a reference to Plato's *Laws* 894 A—

γίγνεται δὴ πάντων γένεσις, ἡνίκ᾽ ἂν τί πάθος ᾖ; δῆλον ὡς ὁπόταν ἀρχὴ λαβοῦσα αὔξην εἰς τὴν δευτέραν ἔλθῃ μετάβασιν, καὶ ἀπὸ ταύτης εἰς τὴν πλησίον, καὶ μέχρι τριῶν ἐλθοῦσα αἴσθησιν σχῇ τοῖς αἰσθανομένοις. μεταβάλλον μὲν οὖν οὕτω καὶ μετακινούμενον γίγνεται πᾶν· ἔστι δὲ ὄντως ὄν, ὁπόταν μένῃ· μεταβαλὸν δὲ εἰς ἄλλην ἕξιν διέφθαρται παντελῶς.

From these citations I conclude that *the Platonic Idea possesses four phases or conditions, whereof the first is opposed to the remaining three as* ὄντως οὐσία *to* γένεσις. As ὄντως ὄν Aristotle calls the Idea αὐτὴ ἡ τοῦ ἑνὸς ἰδέα; and Plato adds that it μένει (= the στάσις of *Soph.* 249 B, C). As γιγνόμενον Aristotle couples it with space of one, two, and three dimensions; and Plato adds that it is developed through these same stages μεταβάλλον καὶ μετακινούμενον (= the[29] κίνησις of *Soph.* 249 A, B).

Thus, on the one hand, the separation between Ideal οὐσία and phenomenal γένεσις, enquired after by the Platonic Parmenides—

Parm. 130 B αὐτὸς σὺ οὕτω διῄρησαι ὡς λέγεις, χωρὶς μὲν εἴδη αὐτὰ ἄττα, χωρὶς δὲ τὰ τούτων αὖ μετέχοντα;—

and affirmed by the εἰδῶν φίλοι—

Soph. 248 A γένεσιν, τὴν δὲ οὐσίαν χωρίς που διελόμενοι λέγετε; ἢ γάρ; Ναί.—

is still retained in Plato's mature ontology; for the Idea ἔστιν ὄντως ὂν ὁπόταν μένῃ· μεταβαλὸν δὲ εἰς ἄλλην ἕξιν διέφθαρται παντελῶς. While, on the other hand, neither the Ideal nor the phenomenal world is complete apart from its correlative; for στάσις and κίνησις, although ἐναντιώτατα ἀλλήλοις, are both essential factors of οὐσία, which is in every case evolved from the single state of the former through the threefold condition of the latter.

There are two further reflections suggested by the passage from the *Laws*, which may be briefly indi-

---

[29] [Alexander] *in Arist. Met.* M. 2. 1077 a 14 ed. Hayduck p. 731, 16 πρότερον γὰρ ἐπὶ μῆκος γίνεται ἡ αὔξησις ἢ ὅλως ἡ κίνησις, ἔπειτα εἰς πλάτος, εἶτα εἰς βάθος.

cated here. (*a*) In the first place, without discussing the details of the context in which that passage is set I may point out that by the ἀρχή of *Laws* 894 A Plato means ψυχή. Thus much is clear from the similarity of the language that follows in 896 A, B—

ἆρα ἔτι ποθοῦμεν μὴ ἱκανῶς δεδεῖχθαι ψυχὴν ταὐτὸν ὂν καὶ τὴν πρώτην γένεσιν καὶ κίνησιν τῶν τε ὄντων καὶ γεγονότων καὶ ἐσομένων καὶ πάντων αὖ τῶν ἐναντίων τούτοις, ἐπειδή γε ἀνεφάνη μεταβολῆς τε καὶ κινήσεως ἁπάσης αἰτία ἅπασιν;—Οὔκ, ἀλλὰ ἱκανώτατα δέδεικται ψυχὴ τῶν πάντων πρεσβυτάτη, φανεῖσά γε ἀρχὴ κινήσεως.

This identification[30] supports my contention that αὐτὸ τὸ ζῷον, the subject of the second clause in the argument from Aristotle's *Psychology*, is not to be distinguished from ψυχή, the subject of the first clause in the same argument; inasmuch as the four stages assigned by the *Psychology* to the αὐτὸ ζῷον are by the *Laws* attributed to ψυχή. (*b*) Secondly, the full phrase ἀρχὴ κινήσεως, which recalls the language of earlier days (*Phaedrus* 245 C πηγὴ καὶ ἀρχὴ κινήσεως), may be taken to include both aspects of ψυχή—the ἠρεμία of its higher, and

---

[30] If it be objected that Aristotle (*vid.* p. 27) uses the term ἀρχὴ to denote not ψυχὴ but the elements of which ψυχὴ is constructed, I answer that the pupil's usage is no voucher for the master's Indeed Aristotle himself (*Psych*. A. 2. 7. 404*b* 24), as we shall see directly, complains that Plato "calls the ἀριθμοὶ εἴδη καὶ ἀρχαί whereas they really are ἐκ τῶν στοιχείων."

the κίνησις of its lower intellectuality. The compiler of the Platonic ὅροι was not far wrong when he defined νόησις as ἀρχὴ ἐπιστήμης, and αἴσθησις as νοῦ κίνησις.

But the mention of the diverse faculties of ψυχὴ reminds us that we have still to analyse the remainder of Aristotle's argument, which treats of them *seriatim*.

iii. The third clause is epitomized by Dr. Jackson as follows—

> We reduce *things* to ἀριθμοί (*i.e.* Ideal Numbers), and therefore to the elements of these ἀριθμοί, *sc.* to 1. 2. 3. 4.
>
> Again, the *processes of mind* are expressed by the same elements, 1. 2. 3. 4.

This interpretation, though furnishing the needed parallelism between subject and object, labours under two serious drawbacks:

(*a*) The στοιχεῖα of the Ideal ἀριθμοὶ are not the numbers 1. 2. 3. 4., but the principles of Identity and Difference, which were technically known by this very name; see, for example,

> *Met.* N. 1. 1087 *b* 14 οἱ τὸ μέγα καὶ τὸ μικρὸν λέγοντες μετὰ τοῦ ἑνὸς τρία ταῦτα στοιχεῖα τῶν ἀριθμῶν.

(β) Either the words εἴδη δ' οἱ ἀριθμοὶ οὗτοι πραγμάτων, or the words οἱ μὲν γὰρ ἀριθμοί .... τὰ δ' αἰσθήσει, become superfluous; the argument is complete without them. Nor do we mend matters much

if we invert the order of these two sentences. For, that transposition granted, the passage will run:—
"And these numbers (*sc.* 1. 2. 3. 4.) are forms of things; for on the one hand the Numbers were known as the absolute Ideas and first principles, and they are constructed out of their elements (*sc.* 1. 2. 3. 4.); while on the other hand things are apprehended—some by νοῦς, some by ἐπιστήμη, some by δόξα, some by αἴσθησις." But that εἴδη δ' οἱ ἀριθμοὶ οὗτοι τῶν πραγμάτων should be followed immediately by οἱ μὲν γὰρ ἀριθμοὶ τὰ εἴδη ... ἐλέγοντο,—a sentence in which both leading words are repeated in a different sense,—is hardly credible.

In the face of these difficulties I should prefer to retain the text unaltered, remarking that if the words οἱ μὲν γὰρ ἀριθμοὶ τὰ εἴδη αὐτὰ καὶ ἀρχαὶ ἐλέγοντο, εἰσὶ δ' ἐκ τῶν στοιχείων had stood alone, they would have been interpreted without fail: "The εἰδητικοὶ ἀριθμοὶ were spoken of as the absolute Ideas and principles, though in point of fact they are compounded of the elements." Moreover, the expression ἐκ τῶν στοιχείων would have been understood here in 404*b* 25 as it was understood a few lines higher up in 404*b* 17—" of the elements ταὐτὸν + θάτερον = οὐσία." Again, it is natural to suppose that the word οὗτοι, added to οἱ ἀριθμοὶ in the last sentence, is intented to connect them with the faculties just enumerated and to distinguish them from the Ideal ἀριθμοί. Lastly, the statement that these four numbers (1. 2. 3. 4.) represent εἴδη τῶν πραγμάτων must balance the statement that the percipient has four modes of cognition symbolically denoted by the same numbers (1. 2. 3. 4.); and since a quasi-spacial account of those modes has been given already (in the words ἐπιστήμην δὲ τὰ δύο· μοναχῶς γὰρ ἐφ᾽ ἕν· τὸν δὲ τοῦ ἐπιπέδου ἀριθμὸν δόξαν, αἴσθησιν δὲ τὸν τοῦ στερεοῦ), it is probable that these εἴδη τῶν πραγμάτων are things in general grouped according to the four stages[31] through which, as we learnt from the second clause, percept Ideas pass into the region of αἴσθησις: certainly the broad meaning thus assigned to the word εἶδος = "class" or "group" is supported by the fact that the article, prefixed to the same word when used above in its technical sense (τὰ εἴδη αὐτά), is here absent. The argument, I take it, may be set out as follows:—

Again, the one . . . . is νοῦς,
       the two . . . . is ἐπιστήμη,
       the no. of the plane (*i.e.* three) is δόξα,
       the no. of the solid (*i.e.* four) is αἴσθησις.

Now, on the one hand (μέν) the Numbers were called the fundamental Ideas of the Platonic system —though, to speak with all precision, they are con-

---

[31] Simplic *in Arist. Psych.* ed. Hayduck p. 29, 12 διῄρουν δὲ τά τε ὄντα οὐ κατὰ πλάτος, ἀλλὰ κατὰ βάθος, εἴς τε τὰ νοητὰ καὶ ἐπιστητὰ καὶ δοξαστὰ καὶ αἰσθητά, καὶ ὁμοίως τὰς γνώσεις εἰς νοῦν καὶ ἐπιστήμην καὶ δόξαν καὶ αἴσθησιν.

structed out of the στοιχεῖα (*sc.* ταὐτὸν + θάτερον = οὐσία) —and they apprehend things by means of the four faculties above mentioned.

On the other hand (δέ) these four numbers (*i.e.* the numbers 1. 2. 3. 4., representing the four faculties) are groups of things.

In brief, Aristotle's point is that the percipient Ideas evolved as aforesaid apprehend by means of four faculties, and that these faculties correspond to four stages in the spacial evolution of the percept Ideas: what those stages are we already know.

The recognition of the planes of consciousness symbolised by these numbers 1. 2. 3. 4. throws light —where light is much needed—upon the use of the technical term δεκάς. Aristotle more than once affirms that certain Idealists continued their Ideal Numbers μέχρι τῆς δεκάδος:

Met. Λ. 8. 1073 a 20 περὶ δὲ τῶν ἀριθμῶν ὁτὲ μὲν ὡς περὶ ἀπείρων λέγουσιν, ὁτὲ δ' ὡς μέχρι τῆς δεκάδος ὡρισμένων.

Ibid. Μ. 8. 1084 a 12 εἰ δὲ πεπερασμένος, μέχρι πόσου; τοῦτο γὰρ δεῖ λέγεσθαι οὐ μόνον ὅτι, ἀλλὰ καὶ διότι. ἀλλὰ μὴν εἰ μέχρι τῆς δεκάδος ὁ ἀριθμός, ὥσπερ τινές φασιν, πρῶτον μὲν ταχὺ ἐπιλείψει τὰ εἴδη· οἷον εἰ ἔστιν ἡ τριὰς αὐτοάνθρωπος, τίς ἔσται ἀριθμὸς αὐτόιππος; αὐτὸ γὰρ ἕκαστος ἀριθμὸς μέχρι δεκάδος.

Ibid. M. 8. 1084 a 29 ἔτι ἄτοπον εἰ ὁ ἀριθμὸς μέχρι τῆς δεκάδος, μᾶλλον τι ὂν τὸ ἓν καὶ εἶδος αὐτῆς τῆς δεκάδος.

Ibid. N. I. 1088 b 10 οἷον ἡ δεκὰς πολύ, εἰ ταύτης μή ἐστι πλεῖον.

Phys. Γ. 6. 206 b 32 μέχρι γὰρ δεκάδος ποιεῖ τὸν ἀριθμόν.

Now the statement that Ideal Numbers were continued μέχρι τῆς δεκάδος is open to two interpretations. On the one hand, it might mean that there are but ten Ideas in the Ideal series. It was, in fact, obviously so understood, or misunderstood, by certain crude followers of the first Academy. Aristotle's evidence on the point is rendered explicit by

[Alex.] *in Arist. Met.* ed. Hayduck p. 700, 27 εἰ γὰρ αἱ ἰδέαι ἀριθμοί, ὁ δ' ἀριθμὸς ἄχρι τῆς δεκάδος ἵσταται, αἱ ἰδέαι ἄρα δέκα.

But to impute such puerility to Plato himself is surely out of the question. Aware that his materials for a comparative study of nature were as yet scanty in the extreme, he probably refrained from delivering any exact dogma with regard to the number of absolute Ideas:

Met. Λ. 8. 1073 a 16 περὶ πλήθους οὐδὲν εἰρήκασιν, ὅ τι καὶ σαφὲς εἰπεῖν.

At most he may have vouchsafed the remark that the Ideas were μύρια, in order to prevent the supposition that they were ἄπειρα. This limitation is possibly alluded to elsewhere by Aristotle:

Met. N. 1. 1088 *b* 11 οἷον ἡ δεκὰς πολύ, εἰ ταύτης μή ἐστι πλεῖον, ἢ τὰ μύρια.

In any case Plato cannot have ignored the palpable absurdity of a system comprising only ten *infimae species*. On the other hand, the phrase μέχρι τῆς δεκάδος is susceptible of a different interpretation. It may imply that each individual Idea contains within itself the perfect number ten. And that this was Plato's real meaning appears from an interesting Aristotelian fragment (ed. Rose 1477 *b* 40) preserved by Philoponus *in Arist. Psych. A.* 2. 7. 404 *b* 18:

λέγει οὖν (Aristotle) φάσκειν αὐτούς (Plato and the Pythagoreans) ὅτι τὰ εἴδη ἀριθμοί εἰσιν, ἀριθμοὶ δὲ δεκαδικοί· ἕκαστον γὰρ τῶν εἰδῶν δεκάδα ἔλεγον.

Recent exegesis has regarded the testimony of Philoponus either as erroneous and without foundation (see Trendelenburg *de an.* ed. 1877 p. 189), or as reliable and important (see Brandis *de perd. Arist. libris* p. 49 *seqq.*). Those who credit the assertion have, however, been put to strange shifts to support their view. Maguire, for example, in *The Platonic Idea* p. 69 *seq.*, obtains his decad in the following fashion: "The Idea as I is the result of II the combination of III the Indefinite and of IV Unity.... The Idea is a Result of a Combination of Two Elements, of which the former indirectly, and the latter directly, rests on an absolute Basis.... That is to say, The IV presupposes The III; The III presupposes The II; The II presupposes The I; while The I is self-sufficing, and verges on the absolute. But, since

$$IV + III + II + I = X,$$

we may see how, in Plato's mind, The Ten denoted not only the highest form, but also the living substance of Supreme Reality." I do not think that we need resort to such subtleties for a satisfactory explanation. If every Ideal Number possesses four phases of consciousness denoted respectively by the numbers 1. 2. 3. 4, then it is evident that in a sense every Ideal Number is the sum of $1 + 2 + 3 + 4$, or, in other words, is a δεκάς.[31a] In short, the problematic use of the term δεκὰς as applied to the Platonic Ideas finds a simple solution in this third clause of the argument from Aristotle's *Psychology*.

The general bearing of that clause may be thus illustrated.[32] We particular men, who fancy ourselves

---

[31a] Philoponus, then, is partially right when he adds (*loc. cit.*) ἀριθμοὶ μὲν οὖν διὰ τοῦτο· δεκαδικοὶ δὲ διὰ τὴν τελειότητα τῶν εἰδῶν. The παντελῶς ὂν of *Soph.* 248 E was found to involve the development of νοῦς into ἐπιστήμη, δόξα, αἴσθησις, and the symbols of these four stages produce the decad, which the Pythagoreans named Παντέλεια (Stob. *Ecl.* I. ed. Wachsmuth i. p. 22, 5).

[32] For the ensuing description cp. Simplic. *in Arist. Psych.* ed. Hayduck p. 29, 2 ἀνῆγον δὲ εἰς τὰς εἰδητικὰς ἀρχὰς καὶ τὰς ψυχικὰς

separate entities, are but the Ideal animal Man regarding itself on the plane of αἴσθησις: what we see is therefore a plurality of men moving in three-dimensional space. When we entertain opinions about things, we rise to a higher level and portray them to ourselves by a kind of mental delineation: they still shape themselves as pluralities, but pluralities moving in two dimensions, a flat and it may be delusive picture of surrounding life. As individuals we are capable of a yet higher method of cognition, namely that of ἐπιστήμη: when a man knows a thing, he so to speak goes "straight to the point" (μοναχῶς γὰρ ἐφ' ἕν) in his intellectual presentation; and though

---

πάσας γιώσεις, τὴν μὲν νοερὰν ὡς καθ' ἕνωσιν ἀμέριστον συναιρουμένην εἰς τὴν μονάδα, τὴν δὲ ἐπιστημονικὴν ὡς ἀνελισσομένην καὶ ὡς ἀπὸ ἑτέρου τοῦ αἰτίου εἰς τὸ αἰτιατὸν προαγομένην, ὡς δὲ καὶ διὰ τὸ ἀπλανὲς καὶ ἀεὶ διὰ τῶν αὐτῶν ὁδεῦον εἰς τὴν δυάδα, τὴν δὲ δόξαν εἰς τὴν τριάδα διὰ τὸ τὴν δύναμιν αὐτῆς μὴ ἐπὶ τὸ αὐτὸ ἀεί, ἀλλὰ τοτὲ μὲν ἐπὶ τὸ ἀληθὲς τοτὲ δὲ ἐπὶ τὸ ψεῦδος κλίνειν, εἰς δὲ τὴν τετράδα τὴν αἴσθησιν διὰ τὸ σωμάτων εἶναι ἀντιληπτικήν. Themist. *in Arist. Psych.* ed. Spengel p. 21, 17 τὸν μὲν νοῦν ἔχειν ἐκ τῆς τοῦ ἑνὸς ἰδέας αὐτήν (sc. τὴν ψυχήν) διωρίζοντο, τὴν δὲ ἐπιστήμην ἐκ τῆς πρώτης δυάδος· ἀφ' ἑνὸς γὰρ ἐφ' ἕν καὶ ἡ ἐπιστήμη· ἀπὸ γὰρ τῶν προτάσεων ἐπὶ τὸ συμπέρασμα, τὴν δόξαν δὲ ἐκ τῆς πρώτης τριάδος, ὅσος ἦν καὶ τοῦ ἐπιπέδου ἀριθμός· τῆς γὰρ δόξης ἤδη καὶ τὸ ἀληθὲς καὶ τὸ ψεῦδος ἐκ τῶν προτάσεων, αἴσθησιν δὲ ἀπὸ τῆς πρώτης τετράδος ἐξ ἧς καὶ ἡ τοῦ στερεοῦ σώματος ἰδέα· περὶ γὰρ τὸ τοιοῦτον σῶμα ἡ αἴσθησις. Sophonias *in Arist. Psych.* ed. Hayduck p. 13, 37 δυὰς γὰρ τὰ ἐπιστημονικὰ τὸ ποθὲν πῇ ὡρισμένως ἔχοντα· τριὰς δὲ ἡ δόξα· τριττὰ γὰρ καὶ τὰ δοξαστὰ διὰ τὸ ἀμφιρρεπές· ἀπὸ δὲ τῆς τετράδος τὴν αἴσθησιν, ὅτι περὶ τὸ σῶμα, ὃ τετράδι συντέθειται.

Aristotle[33] scoffs at those who are content to regard the soul's knowledge as a series of lines, yet the modern science of psychophysics has certainly tended to confirm Plato's acute conjecture. To rise above ἐπιστήμη is impossible for us—

Laws 897 D μὴ τοίνυν ἐξ ἐναντίας οἷον εἰς ἥλιον ἀποβλέποντες, νύκτα ἐν μεσημβρίᾳ ἐπαγόμενοι, ποιησώμεθα τὴν ἀπόκρισιν, ὡς νοῦν ποτὲ θνητοῖς ὄμμασιν ὀψόμενοί τε καὶ γνωσόμενοι ἱκανῶς—

inasmuch as particular thinkers are the Ideal animal actively functioning in the mode of θάτερον, and in the next stage—νόησις—particulars coalesce into the Idea. It is reserved for the Idea itself to enjoy that direct intuition of which the neo-Platonists said[34] νοεῖ οὐ ζητῶν, ἀλλ' ἔχων.

We are now in a position to combine the results of all three clauses and to indicate the advance made by the passage as a whole.

From the critique of the Platonic Parmenides, fittingly supplemented by that of the Eleatic stranger,

---

[33] *Met. M.* 2. 1077 a 29, *Psych. A.* 4. 17. 409 a 5. It is, however, to be observed that in 407 a 29 Aristotle has himself been guilty of much the same conception as that which he ridicules: αἱ δ' ἀποδείξεις καὶ ἀπ' ἀρχῆς, καὶ ἔχουσί πως τέλος, τὸν συλλογισμὸν ἢ τὸ συμπέρασμα· εἰ δὲ μὴ περατοῦνται, ἀλλ' οὐκ ἀνακάμπτουσί γε πάλιν ἐπ' ἀρχήν, προσλαμβάνουσαι δ' ἀεὶ μέσον καὶ ἄκρον εὐθυποροῦσιν.

[34] Plotinus *Enn.* V. i. 4, cp. V. i. 10, V. v. 1.

we had conceived the ground-plan of the universe as a single οὐσία multiplying itself into a series of οὐσίαι. Each οὐσία was a νοητὸν ζῷον, whose nature necessarily comprised two functions; on the one hand a power of passionless thought, that might be named νόησις; on the other hand a power of active and passive thought, that might be named γνῶσις. In the case of the universal οὐσία, νόησις was represented by the supreme Νοῦς; in the case of the series of οὐσίαι, νόησις was represented by the Ideas.

The argument from Aristotle's *Psychology*, reviewed in connection with certain corroborative statements, has amplified this theory as follows:—

(1) Οὐσία is now identified with ψυχή[35]—the single all-embracing ὄν with the παντελὲς ζῷον, the assemblage of partial or Ideal ὄντα with the ἐν μέρους εἴδει ζῷα. The higher and lower mentality, which together formed the οὐσία of a νοητὸν ζῷον, are thus equated with ταὐτὸν and θάτερον, which together form the οὐσία of an Ideal ἔμψυχον. Further, the objects of cognition for any such ἔμψυχον are declared to be the remaining and similarly constructed ἔμψυχα.

(2) Every absolute animal, whether it be the whole cosmic animal or one of the partial and subordinate animals, evolves itself through four phases or con-

---

[35] Cp. Simplicius *in Arist. Psych.* ed. Hayduck, p. 10, 33 οἱ μὲν οὖν Πυθαγόρειοι καὶ Πλάτων οὐσίαν αὐτὴν (*sc.* τὴν ψυχήν) φάσιν.

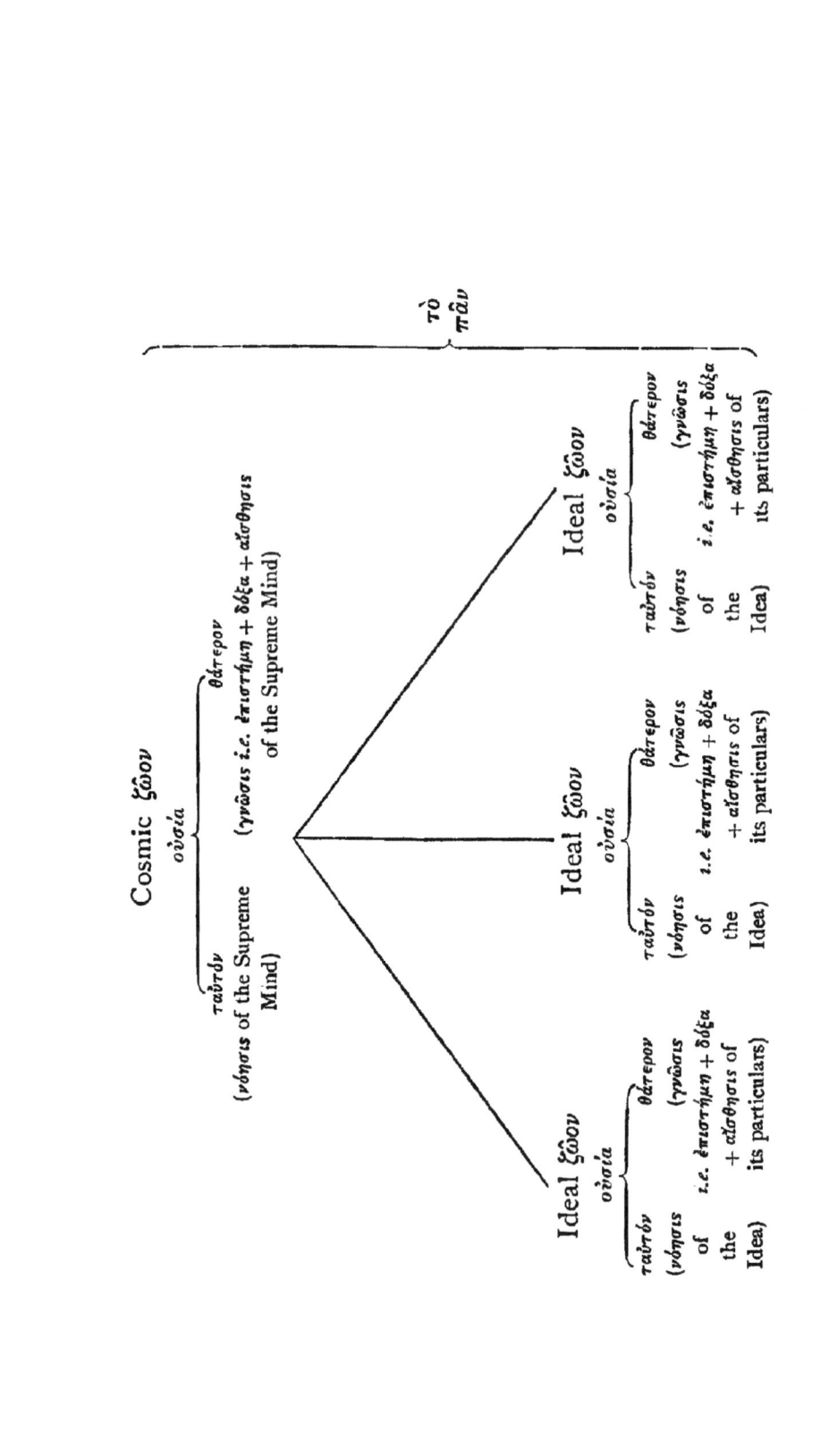

$$
\text{Cosmic } \zetaῷον \left\{ \begin{array}{l} οὐσία \\ \\ \underbrace{ταὐτόν}_{\substack{(νόησις \text{ of the Supreme} \\ \text{Mind})}} \quad \underbrace{θάτερον}_{\substack{(γνῶσις \text{ i.e. } ἐπιστήμη + δόξα + αἴσθησις \\ \text{of the Supreme Mind})}} \end{array} \right\} \tau ὸ\ π ᾶν
$$

Ideal ζῷον
  οὐσία
  ταὐτόν (νόησις of the Idea)
  θάτερον (γνῶσις i.e. ἐπιστήμη + δόξα + αἴσθησις of its particulars)

Ideal ζῷον
  οὐσία
  ταὐτόν (νόησις of the Idea)
  θάτερον (γνῶσις i.e. ἐπιστήμη + δόξα + αἴσθησις of its particulars)

Ideal ζῷον
  οὐσία
  ταὐτόν (νόησις of the Idea)
  θάτερον (γνῶσις i.e. ἐπιστήμη + δόξα + αἴσθησις of its particulars)

ditions, *viz.* (a) the immutable being of ἡ τοῦ ἑνὸς ἰδέα, and (β) the mutable becoming of the same in space of one, two, and three dimensions. Its objects of cognition are again the remaining and similarly developed animals.

(3) Each Idea in its perceptive evolution acquires four planes of consciousness :—

As endowed with νοῦς it νοεῖ,
As passing into ἐπιστήμη it ἐπίσταται,
As passing into δόξα it δοξάζει,
As passing into αἴσθησις it αἰσθάνεται.

Moreover, the object of its perception throughout these four stages is any other Idea, perceived—

by νοῦς as an ἀριθμός ;
by ἐπιστήμη as a μῆκος,
by δόξα as an ἐπίπεδον,
by αἴσθησις as a στερεόν.

Thus the passage as a whole enables us to fill up and complete the outlines of the Platonic scheme.

PART II.

HIGHER AND LOWER MENTALITY.

At the outset of the present enquiry I proposed to analyse certain incidental passages of pregnant meaning in order to obtain some simple and yet adequate formula for the interrelations of Plato's Idealism. This analysis has established the main fact that Mind is operant in two different ways within the limits of Platonic ontology. For, in the first place, Mind is a Unity self-pluralised into a conclave of Minds, which are *objective*—*i.e.* really existent—Ideas. And in the second place, on pain of forfeiting its claim to real existence, Mind passes everywhere out of its own condition of permanent and immutable thought into the transitory and mutable phases of knowledge, opinion, sensation, thereby producing *subjective*—*i.e.* phenomenally existent—particulars. In the words of Proklos: πᾶσα ἡ τῶν ψυχῶν τάξις εἰς δύο ταύτας ἀνήρτηται πηγάς, τήν τε δημιουργικὴν καὶ τὴν ζωογονικήν.[36]

So far the outlines of the theory. It remains to

---

[36] Proklos *in Tim.* 319 A.

indicate the ethical colouring of the whole. But before attempting this further task, it will be well to secure due perspective by emphasising afresh the salient points of view. I shall, therefore, in the present chapter endeavour to illustrate from the Platonic dialogues the contrast thus formulated between the *objective* and *subjective* aspects of Mind, in the hope that each successive illustration, while exhibiting Plato's technical consistency in the use of non-technical terms, may bring into clearer light the moral significance of his design.

§ I. *Purpose and Necessity.*

Timaeus 47 E discriminates (*a*) τὰ διὰ νοῦ δεδημιουργημένα from (*b*) τὰ δι᾽ ἀνάγκης γιγνόμενα, and declares that the universe is the combined product of both: μεμιγμένη γὰρ οὖν ἡ τοῦδε τοῦ κόσμου γένεσις ἐξ ἀνάγκης τε καὶ νοῦ συστάσεως ἐγεννήθη.

Now (*a*) the creations of νοῦς, as we learnt from the *Parmenides*, comprise a series of subordinate Minds called the Ideas, which are unified in a single supreme Mind conceived as their basis and groundwork. Again, (*b*) τὰ δι᾽ ἀνάγκης γιγνόμενα are the results brought about by the necessary passage of the said Minds from the higher mode of "being" into the lower mode of "becoming"; and this lapse, this deviation, is as such[37] referred in the *Timaeus* to ἡ πλανωμένη αἰτία. It is clear, therefore, that Plato, when he contrasts τὰ διὰ νοῦ δεδημιουργημένα with τὰ δι' ἀνάγκης γιγνόμενα, is describing just those two aspects of Mind which I have termed "objective" and "subjective." And we are confronted by the question: on what principle of distinction is the latter and not the former assigned to ἀνάγκη?

The reason of the change is not, I think, far to seek. It is ἀνάγκη that the supreme Mind should pass from the ταὐτότης of νοῦς into the ἑτερότης of ἐπιστήμη, δόξα, αἴσθησις. It is ἀνάγκη, too, that the subordinate Ideal Minds should similarly pass from perfect to imperfect thought. But it is *not ἀνάγκη* that the supreme Mind should multiply itself into the Ideas. That process of objective pluralisation is never in Plato described as ἀναγκαῖον. It is on the contrary directly referred to βούλησις, the very opposite[38] of ἀνάγκη.

In proof of this contention I may cite first *Tim.*

---

[37] Mr. Archer-Hind seems to me ill-advised in stating (ed. *Tim.* p. 167 n.) that "Plato calls ἀνάγκη the πλανωμένη αἰτία, because, though working strictly in obedience to a certain law, it is for the most part as inscrutable to us as if it acted from arbitrary caprice." The term πλανωμένη surely denotes nothing more than *deviation*, and is the equivalent of θάτερον as opposed to ταὐτόν.

[38] For βούλησις)(ἀνάγκη cp. *Crat.* 420 D where τὸ κατὰ τὴν βούλησιν γιγνόμενον is opposed to τὸ ἀναγκαῖον καὶ ἀντίτυπον, παρὰ τὴν βούλησιν ὄν.

29 E—premising that the supreme νοῦς, which in *Phileb.* 28 A—31 A is the αἰτία τῆς μίξεως, must be identified with the θεὸς to whom in the *Timaeus* precisely the same function is allotted:—

(ὁ τὸ πᾶν τόδε ξυνιστὰς) πάντα ὅτι μάλιστα γενέσθαι ἐβουλήθη παραπλήσια ἑαυτῷ. ταύτην δὴ γενέσεως καὶ κόσμου μάλιστ' ἄν τις ἀρχὴν κυριωτάτην παρ' ἀνδρῶν φρονίμων ἀποδεχόμενος ὀρθότατα ἀποδέχοιτ' ἄν. βουληθεὶς γὰρ ὁ θεὸς ἀγαθὰ μὲν πάντα, φλαῦρον δὲ μηδὲν εἶναι κατὰ δύναμιν, οὕτω δὴ πᾶν ὅσον ἦν ὁρατὸν παραλαβὼν οὐχ ἡσυχίαν ἄγον ἀλλὰ κινούμενον πλημμελῶς καὶ ἀτάκτως, εἰς τάξιν αὐτὸ ἤγαγεν ἐκ τῆς ἀταξίας, ἡγησάμενος ἐκεῖνο τούτου πάντως ἄμεινον. (29 E—30 A).

In this paragraph logical analysis lays before us the conception of a supreme Mind brought face to face with a visible chaos. Thus far we are concerned only with ἀνάγκη, which compels νοῦς to degenerate into αἴσθησις,[39] but does not determine under what forms such αἴσθησις shall work. At this point, however, a new element is announced: the supreme Mind

---

[39] *Laws* 818 A ἔοικεν ὁ τὸν θεὸν πρῶτον παροιμιασάμενος (cp. *ibid.* 741 A, *Protag.* 345 D) εἰς ταῦτα ἀποβλέψας εἰπεῖν ὡς οὐδὲ θεὸς ἀνάγκῃ μή ποτε φανῇ μαχόμενος, ὅσαι θεῖαί γε, οἶμαι, τῶν ἀναγκῶν εἰσίν, κ.τ.λ. Similarly the author of the *Epinomis* (? Xenokrates) 982 B ἡ ψυχῆς δὲ ἀνάγκη νοῦν κεκτημένης ἁπασῶν ἀναγκῶν πολὺ μεγίστη γίγνοιτ' ἄν· ἄρχουσα γὰρ ἀλλ' οὐκ ἀρχομένη νομοθετεῖ.

is said to reduce the confusion to order; and this codification of anarchy, this marshalling of motion, is distinctly ascribed to divine βούλησις. If then it can be shown that εἰς τάξιν ἄγειν τὸ ὁρατὸν ἐκ τῆς ἀταξίας was the recognised function of the Ideal series, it will be justly urged that the existence of this series postulates a continued exercise of volition on the part of the supreme Mind.

Phileb. 16 C—17 A informs us that confusion is reduced to order by the interposition of a definite number of species between the one genus and the indefinite plurality of particulars. These species are the πολλά which connect the ἕν with the ἄπειρον, and *ipso facto* distinguish Dialectic from Eristic. We must not be satisfied, says Sokrates, μέχριπερ ἂν τὸ κατ' ἀρχὰς ἓν μὴ ὅτι ἓν καὶ πολλὰ καὶ ἄπειρά ἐστι μόνον ἴδῃ τις, ἀλλὰ καὶ ὁπόσα.

The method is exemplified by the conduct of the Creator both in *Tim.* 53 B—

> ὅτε δ' ἐπεχειρεῖτο κοσμεῖσθαι τὸ πᾶν, πῦρ πρῶτον καὶ ὕδωρ καὶ γῆν καὶ ἀέρα, ἴχνη μὲν ἔχοντα αὐτῶν ἄττα, παντάπασί γε μὴν διακείμενα ὥσπερ εἰκὸς ἔχειν ἅπαν, ὅταν ἀπῇ τινὸς θεός, οὕτω δὴ τότε πεφυκότα ταῦτα πρῶτον διεσχηματίσατο εἴδεσί τε καὶ ἀριθμοῖς.—

and in *Tim.* 69 B—

> ταῦτα ἀτάκτως ἔχοντα ὁ θεὸς ἐν ἑκάστῳ τε αὐτῷ πρὸς αὑτὸ καὶ πρὸς ἄλληλα συμμετρίας ἐνεποίη-

σεν, ὅσας τε καὶ ὅπῃ δυνατὸν ἦν ἀνάλογα καὶ σύμμετρα εἶναι. τότε γὰρ οὔτε τούτων ὅσον μὴ τύχῃ τι μετεῖχεν, οὔτε τὸ παράπαν ὀνομάσαι τῶν νῦν ὀνομαζομένων ἀξιόλογον ἦν οὐδέν, οἷον πῦρ καὶ ὕδωρ καὶ εἴ τι τῶν ἄλλων· ἀλλὰ πάντα ταῦτα πρῶτον διεκόσμησεν, ἔπειτ' ἐκ τούτων πᾶν τόδε ξυνεστήσατο, ζῷον ἓν ζῷα ἔχον τὰ πάντα ἐν αὑτῷ θνητὰ ἀθάνατά τε.

But its application to Idealism will be discerned most clearly from the latter part of the *Parmenides*. The second hypothesis of that dialectical exercise educes, among others, the following results:—

ἓν εἰ ἔστιν, *i.e.* If ἓν participates in οὐσία, then—

(α) ἓν ὄν is a *Whole* comprising *Parts*, whereof each Part is itself a ἓν ὄν comprising *lesser parts*; and by continuing this process of subdivision we may show that the original ἓν ὄν is ἄπειρον τὸ πλῆθος. (142 C— 143 A).

(β) ἕν (not ἓν ὄν, but ἓν conceived apart from οὐσία) is an undivided unity. The possession of οὐσία, however, forces ἓν into combination with τὸ ἕτερον, and occasions the production of συζυγίαι, which may be regarded either as couplets or as triplets, according as we fix our attention on any two of their three factors, or add the third which completes the given triunity

$$\underbrace{\underset{ἕν}{}\underset{ἕτερον}{}}_{οὐσία}$$

Further, the interaction of such factors produces every imaginable number; and we conclude—Εἰ ἄρα ἔστιν ἕν, ἀνάγκη καὶ ἀριθμὸν εἶναι. Ἀνάγκη. Ἀλλὰ μὴν ἀριθμοῦ γε ὄντος πόλλ' ἂν εἴη καὶ πλῆθος ἄπειρον τῶν ὄντων. (143 A—144 A).

(γ) Every ἀριθμὸς participates in οὐσία, and has μόρια, viz. units, which likewise participate in οὐσία. Thus the original ἓν ὂν is not an indivisible Whole, but a Whole that has Parts and is equal to the sum of its Parts. τὸ ἓν ἄρ' αὐτὸ κεκερματισμένον ὑπὸ τῆς οὐσίας πολλά τε καὶ ἄπειρα τὸ πλῆθός ἐστι. (144 A—144 E).

(δ) Lastly, τὸ ἓν may be called πέρας and πεπερασμένον in so far as it is a περιέχον ὅλον. Hence τὸ ἓν ἄρα ὂν[40] ἕν τέ ἐστί που καὶ πολλά, καὶ ὅλον καὶ μόρια, καὶ πεπερασμένον καὶ ἄπειρον πλήθει. (144 E—145 A).

Again, the fourth hypothesis of the *Parmenides* maintains these propositions:—

ἓν εἰ ἔστιν (*i.e.* If ἓν participates in οὐσία), then—

(α) On the one hand τἆλλα, being ἄλλα τοῦ ἑνός, are not ἕν. On the other hand τἆλλα μετέχει πῃ τοῦ ἑνὸς in virtue of possessing μόρια, which are μόρια τοῦ ὅλου τε καὶ ἑνός.

---

[40] Heindorf, Bekker, Schleiermacher, and the Zurich edd. wrongly bracket the word ὄν: it is just this possession of οὐσία which renders possible the subdivision of τὸ ἕν,—apart from οὐσία it would be indivisible.

Thus we posit μία τις ἰδέα καὶ ἕν τι, ὃ καλοῦμεν ὅλον, ἐξ ἁπάντων ἓν τέλειον γεγονός (157 D, E), and affirm that it is composed of πολλὰ μόρια which serve to link τἄλλα with the ἓν ὅλον τέλειον. (157 B—157 E).

(β) Both the ὅλον and each μόριον may be said μετέχειν τοῦ ἑνός, and therefore to be ἕτερα τοῦ ἑνός. And ἡ ἑτέρα φύσις τοῦ εἴδους will ever be ἄπειρον πλήθει. (157 E—158 C).

(γ) Lastly, τὰ ἄλλα τοῦ ἑνός, when combined with τὸ ἕν, give rise to a third class of existences, viz. τὰ μόρια, which πέρας πάρεσχε πρὸς ἄλληλα, thereby limiting the ἀπειρία inherent in τὰ ἄλλα and establishing certain fixed relations with τὸ ὅλον. (158 C—158 D).

The argumentation of these two hypotheses reiterates the lesson of the *Philebus*. Between ἓν ὄν and πλῆθος ἄπειρον τῶν ὄντων must be ranged a series of πολλὰ ὄντα related to the former as ἀριθμοὶ to ἕν or as μόρια to ὅλον, to the latter as πέρας παρέχοντα to ἄπειρα. These conditions being granted, knowledge becomes a possibility (*Parm.* 155 D). We may well follow Dr. Jackson when in this class of intermediates he recognises the Ideas of Plato's own ontology.[41]

It appears, then, that both in the *Philebus* and in the *Parmenides* the Ideas are regarded as a bond between the single objective Mind and the indefinity

---

[41] *The Journal of Philology*, xi, 318.

of subjective phenomena, their prerogative being to introduce the πέρας of the former into the ἀπειρία of the latter. The words of Aetios[42] are strictly accurate:

ἰδέα ἐστὶν οὐσία ἀσώματος, αἰτία τῶν οἷα ἐστὶν αὐτὴ καὶ παράδειγμα τῆς τῶν κατὰ φύσιν ἐχόντων αἰσθητῶν ὑποστάσεως, αὐτὴ μὲν ὑφεστῶσα καθ' ἑαυτήν [ἕν], εἰκονίζουσα δὲ τὰς ἀμόρφους ὕλας καὶ αἰτία γιγνομένη τῆς τούτων διατάξεως.

And since this very introduction of order into disorder is stated in the *Timaeus* to be the outcome of the divine intent, it results that the objective pluralisation of νοῦς which produces the Ideal νοήματα is due to θεία βούλησις, and is rightly opposed[43] to the subjective action of ἀνάγκη or ἡ πλανωμένη αἰτία. As *Tim.* 68 E puts it:

χρὴ δύ' αἰτίας εἴδη διορίζεσθαι, τὸ μὲν ἀναγκαῖον, τὸ δὲ θεῖον.

And here—lest we should misconstrue Plato's deliberate recognition of βούλησις into an acknowledgement of despotic caprice on the part of the Creator—

---

[42] Stob. *Ecl.* I. xii. 1 a, ed. Wachsmuth i. p. 134, 9 ff.

[43] Unless, indeed, we hold that Plato like Aristotle recognised a hypothetical ἀνάγκη. The latter author sometimes (*e.g. Psych.* B. 8. 10. 420 b 19 seq.) distinguishes ἀναγκαῖον from ἕνεκα τοῦ εὖ, but elsewhere (*e.g. de part. an. A.* 1. 642 a 32 ἢ δ' ἀνάγκη ὁτὲ μὲν σημαίνει ὅτι εἰ ἐκεῖνο ἔσται τὸ οὗ ἕνεκα, ταῦτα ἀνάγκη ἐστὶν ἔχειν, ὁτὲ δέ κ.τ.λ.) admits a necessity of a conditional or hypothetical sort. In the second sense Plato's Ideal series would be itself ἀναγκαῖον.

let us recall the tenor of *Tim.* 41 B. In that passage ὁ τόδε τὸ πᾶν γεννήσας addressing the θεοὶ θεῶν assures them of endless life:

οὔ τι μὲν δὴ λυθήσεσθέ γε οὐδὲ τεύξεσθε θανάτου μοίρας, τῆς ἐμῆς βουλήσεως μείζονος ἔτι δεσμοῦ καὶ κυριωτέρου λαχόντες ἐκείνων, οἷς ὅτ' ἐγίγνεσθε ξυνεδεῖσθε.

Now the bonds wherewith the θεοὶ θεῶν had been bound at birth were those of ψυχὴ and ζωή: cp.

Tim. 38 E δεσμοῖς ἐμψύχοις σώματα δεθέντα ζῶα ἐγεννήθη.

Ibid. 40 B ζῶα θεῖα ὄντα καὶ ἀίδια καὶ κατὰ ταὐτὰ ἐν ταὐτῷ στρεφόμενα.

And it has been shown that ζωὴ and ψυχὴ are the predicates of οὐσία when it is in a state of motion. I infer that the μείζων δεσμὸς will be that which is predicable of οὐσία when it is in a state of rest, namely νόησις. The inference is supported by *Tim.* 48 A, which denies the demotic creed οὐδεὶς ἀνάγκης μεῖζον ἰσχύει νόμος,[44] affirming that νοῦς is lord even over ἀνάγκη.

Thus *Tim.* 41 B corroborates the coextension of βούλησις with νόησις,—inasmuch as it attributes to

---

[44] *Frag. Trag. adesp.* 421 N. cp. Eur. *Alk.* 965—
κρεῖσσον οὐδὲν Ἀνάγκας
ηὗρον.

the former[45] a supremacy which is elsewhere ascribed to nothing less than the latter,—and by the same means provides the needed assurance that we are dealing with no arbitrary display of divine volition, but with the unvarying purpose of a Being whose eternal aim is the multiplication of his own inherent qualities. Plotinus has read Plato aright:

ἡ δὲ θέλησις οὐκ ἄλογος ἦν, οὐδὲ τοῦ εἰκῆ, οὐδ' ὡς ἐπῆλθεν αὐτῷ, ἀλλ' ὡς ἔδει, ὡς οὐδενὸς ὄντος ἐκεῖ εἰκῆ.[46]

These conclusions accord with the wording of 41 A, where the supreme θεὸς speaks of the handiwork of the θεοὶ θεῶν, sc. the τρία θνητὰ γένη—

ἃ δι' ἐμοῦ γενόμενα ἄλυτα ἐμοῦ γε μὴ ἐθέλοντος· τὸ μὲν οὖν δὴ δεθὲν πᾶν λυτόν, τό γε μὴν καλῶς ἁρμοσθὲν καὶ ἔχον εὖ λύειν ἐθέλειν κακοῦ.

That is, the Creator—were he κακός, not ἀγαθός—could, by ceasing to will the existence of the Ideas, at a single blow abolish their dependent γενόμενα.[47] The security that he will not do so lies in the ethical character of his fundamental attributes.

---

[45] The correspondence in point of diction with *Cratylus* 403 c is remarkable. Δεσμὸς ζώῳ ὁτῳοῦν, ὥστε μένειν ὁπουοῦν, πότερος ἰσχυρότερός ἐστιν, ἀνάγκη ἢ ἐπιθυμία. Πολὺ διαφέρει, ὦ Σώκρατες, ἡ ἐπιθυμία.

[46] *Enn.* VI. viii. 18

[47] Cp. *Tim.* 32 c ἄλυτον ὑπό του ἄλλου πλὴν ὑπὸ τοῦ ξυνδήσαντος γενέσθαι.

The moral issues of the doctrine thus elicited are of no trivial order. To follow them out to any length would at this stage of my argument be premature. I shall have occasion to revert to them in the sequel. Here it must suffice to say that the equation βούλησις = νόησις confines all true volition to the Ideal world. For if neither knowledge nor opinion nor sensation, but pure thought alone, be designated as the seat of will, it follows that the unit of voluntary action is no longer the particular but the νοητὸν ζῶον, since nothing short of the νοητὸν ζῶον possesses the prerequisite νόησις.

Turning next from τὰ διὰ νοῦ δεδημιουργημένα to τὰ δι' ἀνάγκης γιγνόμενα (*Tim.* 47 E), we find that Plato regards the degradation whereby Mind lapses from the mode of Identity into that of Diversity as a necessary transition, taking place perforce. The Creator in *Tim.* 35 A combines the psychic ingredients—τὴν θατέρου φύσιν δύσμικτον οὖσαν εἰς ταὐτὸν ξυναρμόττων βίᾳ. The substantive ἀνάγκη and the adjective ἀναγκαῖος are applied, *primarily* to the appearance of Mind in the three lower planes, or in popular parlance to the incarnation of ψυχή, *e.g.*—

Tim. 42 A ὁπότε δὴ σώμασιν ἐμφυτευθεῖεν ἐξ ἀνάγκης (αἱ ψυχαί) κ.τ.λ.

Ibid. 68 E ταῦτα δὴ πάντα τότε ταύτῃ πεφυκότα ἐξ ἀνάγκης ὁ τοῦ καλλίστου τε καὶ ἀρίστου δημιουργὸς ἐν τοῖς γιγνομένοις παρελάμβανεν κ.τ.λ.—

and *secondarily* to the states consequent upon that incarnation, whether they be physical laws, *e.g.*—

Tim. 79 B κατὰ ταύτην τὴν ἀνάγκην πᾶν περιελαυννόμενον κ.τ.λ.

Ibid. 68 B ὧν μήτε τινὰ ἀνάγκην μήτε τὸν εἰκότα λόγον κ.τ.λ.—

bodily dispositions, *e.g.*—

Tim. 75 A ἡ γὰρ ἐξ ἀνάγκης γιγνομένη καὶ ξυντρεφομένη φύσις οὐδαμῇ προσδέχεται πυκνὸν ὀστοῦν κ.τ.λ.

Ibid. 77 A τὴν δὲ ζωὴν ἐν πυρὶ καὶ πνεύματι ξυνέβαινεν ἐξ ἀνάγκης ἔχειν αὐτῷ.—

sensory impulses, *e.g.*—

Tim. 42 A πρῶτον μὲν αἴσθησιν ἀναγκαῖον εἴη μίαν πᾶσιν ἐκ βιαίων παθημάτων ξύμφυτον γίγνεσθαι.

Ibid. 89 B τῶν ἐξ ἀνάγκης παθημάτων.—

emotional concomitants, *e.g.*—

Tim. 69 C—D ἄλλο τε εἶδος ἐν αὐτῷ ψυχῆς προσῳκοδόμουν τὸ θνητόν, δεινὰ καὶ ἀναγκαῖα ἐν ἑαυτῷ παθήματα ἔχον, πρῶτον μὲν ἡδονὴν ... ἔπειτα λύπας ... ἔτι δ' αὖ θάρρος καὶ φόβον ... αἰσθήσει δὲ ἀλόγῳ καὶ ἐπιχειρητῇ παντὸς ἔρωτι ξυγκερασάμενοι ταῦτα ἀναγκαίως τὸ θνητὸν γένος ξυνέθεσαν. καὶ διὰ ταῦτα δὴ σεβόμενοι μιαίνειν τὸ θεῖον, ὅ τι μὴ πᾶσα ἦν ἀνάγκη κ.τ.λ.—

or the broader conditions of morality in general, e g —

> Theaet. 176 A ἀλλ' οὔτ' ἀπολέσθαι τὰ κακὰ δυνατόν, ὦ Θεόδωρε· ὑπεναντίον γάρ τι τῷ ἀγαθῷ ἀεὶ εἶναι ἀνάγκη. οὔτ' ἐν θεοῖς αὐτὰ ἱδρύσθαι, τὴν δὲ θνητὴν φύσιν καὶ τόνδε τὸν τόπον περιπολεῖ ἐξ ἀνάγκης.

This usage of the word and its derivatives is peculiar to Plato, though it was seemingly prefigured by Empedokles, who held that the essence of Ἀνάγκη lay in the combination of Νεῖκος and Φιλία—

> Simplic. in Arist. Phys. ed. Diels p 197, 10 Ἐμπεδοκλῆς . . συνεκορύφωσε τὴν τοῦ νείκους καὶ τῆς φιλίας (ἐναντίωσιν) . . εἰς μονάδα τὴν τῆς ἀνάγκης.
>
> Hippolyt. Ref. vii. 29 Ἀνάγκην καλῶν τὴν ἐξ ἑνὸς εἰς πολλὰ κατὰ τὸ Νεῖκος καὶ ἐκ πολλῶν εἰς ἓν κατὰ τὴν Φιλίαν μεταβολήν.—

and spoke of the punitive incarnation of the heavenly beings as Ἀνάγκης χρῆμα.

To sum up. Plato recognises both an objective and a subjective aspect of Mind. In the former he discerns the *purposive* pluralisation of unitary thought; in the latter the decadence *necessarily* attached to the movement of every real intelligence. As to the relative importance of these two there can be no question: τὸν δὲ νοῦ καὶ ἐπιστήμης ἐραστὴν ἀνάγκη τὰς τῆς ἔμφρονος φύσεως αἰτίας πρώτας μεταδιώκειν, ὅσαι δὲ ὑπ' ἄλλων μὲν κινουμένων, ἕτερα δὲ ἐξ ἀνάγκης κινούντων γίγνονται, δευτέρας[48] (*Tim.* 46 E). Hermes puts the matter in a nutshell when he says[49]—πρόνοια θεία τάξις, ἀνάγκη προνοίᾳ ὑπηρέτις.

§ II. *Identity and Difference.*

An alternative method of notation for the same two aspects of Mind may be found in the quasi-technical terms ταὐτὸν and θάτερον. Hitherto I have used these symbols to betoken respectively the one higher and the three lower planes of psychic existence, whether conceived as actively cognising or as passively cognised; and I have secured provisional consistency by adhering strictly to the statement that every αὐτὸ ζῷον unites in itself ταὐτὸν the mode of pure thought with θάτερον the mode of knowledge, opinion, sensation. It seems, however, desirable to justify this procedure by probing the matter somewhat more deeply, in view of a certain not unnatural tendency to confuse the issues of this terminology with the implications of the antithesis ἓν καὶ πολλά.

To begin with, it must be kept steadily in mind that we are employing *neither* pair of opposites in

---

[48] Cp. Chalcidius *in Plat. Tim.* 41 E ed. Wrobel p. 203 "iuxta Platonem praecedit providentia, sequitur fatum," p. 204 "et divina quidem atque intellegibilia quaeque his proxima sunt secundum providentiam solam (fiunt), naturalia vero et corporea iuxta fatum."

[49] Stob. *Ecl.* I. xli. 1. ed. Wachsmuth i. p. 277, 15.

its widest acceptation. For the *Sophist*, raising the question τί ποτ' αὖ νῦν οὕτως εἰρήκαμεν τό τε ταὐτὸν καὶ θάτερον; (254 E), makes answer that these signs denote general relations applicable to all things in heaven and earth. And in like manner the *Philebus*, declaring the conjunction of unity and multiplicity to be τῶν λόγων αὐτῶν ἀθάνατόν τι καὶ ἀγήρων πάθος (15 D), states that

ἓν καὶ πολλὰ ὑπὸ λόγων γιγνόμενα περιτρέχειν πάντῃ καθ' ἕκαστον τῶν λεγομένων ἀεὶ καὶ πάλαι καὶ νῦν.

Our business then is not with the broad logical sense of these words, but rather with their narrower metaphysical meaning. And the restriction thus imported assumes the following specific form:—

(A) In the Platonic ψυχογονία the term ταὐτὸν is taken to denote that which does not, θάτερον that which does, depart *from its own identity*. It is true that Parmenidean precision might have desiderated the full phrase ταὐτὸν ἑαυτῷ as opposed to ἕτερον ἑαυτοῦ; compare *e.g.*

Parm. 146 A καὶ μὴν ταὐτόν γε δεῖ εἶναι αὐτὸ ἑαυτῷ καὶ ἕτερον ἑαυτοῖ κ.τ.λ.

Ibid. 146 C τὸ ἑτέρωθι ὂν αὐτὸ ἑαυτοῦ ἐν τῷ αὐτῷ ὄντος ἑαυτῷ οὐκ ἀνάγκη αὐτὸ ἑαυτοῦ ἕτερον εἶναι, εἴπερ καὶ ἑτέρωθι ἔσται; Ἔμοιγε δοκεῖ.

But for technical purposes it was obviously convenient to adopt a shortened symbolism, all ambiguity being avoided by the explicit reference of ταὐτὸν and θάτερον to a single οὐσία. Thus the metaphysical limits the logical usage in the following respect. Whereas the logician—appraising words at their current price—predicates both ταὐτὸν and θάτερον of any thing or aggregate of things, whether real or phenomenal, on the ground that it is the same as itself and different from all else, the metaphysician—fixing the intrinsic value of the terms by a reference to the unvarying standard of οὐσία—assigns ταὐτὸν to ὄντως ὄντα and θάτερον to γιγνόμενα as inalienable characteristics, inasmuch as every ὄντως ὂν abides in eternal self-sameness, while every γιγνόμενον is the fleeting projection of some permanent being[50]—πρὸς τἀληθινὸν ἀφωμοιωμένον ἕτερον τοιοῦτον (*Soph.* 240 A).

Now if all that lapses not from the identity of ὄντως οὐσία be fitly termed ταὐτόν, the domain of ταὐτότης will comprise on the one hand (α) the supreme Mind; for the ordering of the chaotic universe could not impair the moveless calm of intelligence:

Tim. 42 E ὁ μὲν δή (θεός, *i.e.* νοῦς) ἅπαντα ταῦτα
  διατάξας ἔμενεν ἐν τῷ ἑαυτοῦ κατὰ τρόπον ἤθει·
  μένοντος δὲ νοήσαντες οἱ παῖδες κ.τ.λ.—

and on the other hand (β) the series of Ideal Minds; for they are as stable as the goodness that gave them birth:

---

[50] Vid. *e.g. Tim.* 52 C.

Tim. 52 A ὁμολογητέον ἓν μὲν εἶναι τὸ κατὰ ταὐτὰ εἶδος ἔχον, ἀγένητον καὶ ἀνώλεθρον, οὔτε εἰς ἑαυτὸ εἰσδεχόμενον ἄλλο ἄλλοθεν οὔτε αὐτὸ εἰς ἄλλο ποι ἰόν, ἀόρατον δὲ καὶ ἄλλως ἀναίσθητον, τοῦτο ὃ δὴ νόησις εἴληχεν ἐπισκοπεῖν.

The latter as comprehended by the former constitute the παραδείγματος εἶδος, νοητὸν καὶ ἀεὶ κατὰ ταὐτὰ ὄν (*Tim.* 48 E).

Again, if all that lapses from the identity of ὄντως οὐσία be fitly termed ἕτερον, the domain of ἑτερότης will comprise on the one hand (α) the visible manifestation of the supreme Mind, and on the other hand (β) the visible manifestations of the Ideal Minds. The latter as comprehended by the former constitute the μίμημα παραδείγματος, γένεσιν ἔχον καὶ ὁρατόν (*Tim.* 49 A).

In short, the terms ταὐτὸν and θάτερον in their *primary* ontological significance serve to discriminate the ἀντίστοιχα of *Tim.* 27 D—29 D:—

οὐσία, *the province of* ἀλήθεια. 29 C.	γένεσις *the province of* πίστις. 29 C.
τὸ ὂν ἀεί, γένεσιν δὲ οὐκ ἔχον (27 D)	τὸ γιγνόμενον μὲν ἀεί, ὂν δὲ οὐδέποτε (27 D)
τὸ κατὰ ταὐτὰ ἔχον (28 A)	τὸ γεγονός (28 B)
τὸ κατὰ ταὐτὰ καὶ ὡσαύτως ἔχον (29 A)	τὸ γεγονός (29 A)
τὸ ἀΐδιον (29 A)	τὸ γεγονός (29 A)

τὸ νοήσει μετὰ λόγου περιληπτόν, ἀεὶ κατὰ ταὐτὰ ὄν (28 A)	τὸ δόξῃ μετ' αἰσθήσεως ἀλόγου δοξαστόν, γιγνόμενον καὶ ἀπολλύμενον, ὄντως δὲ οὐδέποτε ὄν (28 A)
τὸ λόγῳ καὶ φρονήσει περιληπτὸν καὶ κατὰ ταὐτὰ ἔχον (29 A)	δόξῃ περιληπτὰ μετ' αἰσθήσεως γιγνόμενα καὶ γεννητά (28 B)
τὸ μόνιμον καὶ βέβαιον καὶ μετὰ νοῦ καταφανές (29 B)	τὸ πρὸς μὲν ἐκεῖνο ἀπεικασθέν, ὂν δὲ εἰκών (29 C)

There are, moreover, certain *secondary* applications of the same terms, of which brief mention may here be made. For since ταὐτὸν and θάτερον correspond to οὐσία and γένεσις, each to each, they may by a slight extension of usage designate also the essential properties of οὐσία and γένεσις.

Thus (a) ταὐτὸν connotes *rest*, θάτερον *motion*:

Tim. 57 E στάσιν μὲν ἐν ὁμαλότητι, κίνησιν δὲ εἰς ἀνωμαλότητα ἀεὶ τιθῶμεν· αἰτία δὲ ἀνισότης αὖ τῆς ἀνωμάλου φύσεως. (That ἀνισότης here = ἡ θατέρου φύσις is clear from its employment in Arist. *Met.* B. 4. 1001 b 23, N. 1. 1087 b 4 ff., 1088 a 15, 2. 1088 b 32, 1089 b 6 ff., 5. 1092 a 29).

Arist. *Phys.* Γ. 2. 201 b 19 δῆλον δὲ σκοποῦσιν ὡς τιθέασιν αὐτὴν ἔνιοι, ἑτερότητα καὶ ἀνισότητα καὶ τὸ μὴ ὂν φάσκοντες εἶναι τὴν κίνησιν (cp. Met. K. 9. 1066 a 10).[51]

So in the disputed passage *Tim.* 74 A τῇ θατέρου προσχρώμενος ἐν αὐτοῖς ὡς μέσῃ ἐνισταμένῃ δυνάμει, κινήσεως καὶ κάμψεως ἕνεκα it is not the "number of parts" that is insisted on, but rather their mobility and flexibility—τῷ ἀρχὰς ἔχειν κινήσεως ἀπό τινος ἐν ταῖς καμπαῖς as Aristotle has it (*Met.* Z. 16. 1040 b 12).[52]

The rationale of this usage may be found in *Cratylus* 439 E (εἰ δὲ ἀεὶ ὡσαύτως ἔχει καὶ τὸ αὐτό ἐστι, πῶς ἂν τοῦτό γε μεταβάλλοι ἢ κινοῖτο, μηδὲν ἐξιστάμενον τῆς αὐτοῦ ἰδέας; Οὐδαμῶς) as contrasted with Arist. *Psych.* A. 3. 8. 406 b 12 (πᾶσα κίνησις ἔκστασίς ἐστι τοῦ κινουμένου ᾗ κινεῖται), or in *Parm* 145 E—146 A:

Ἕστηκε μέν που, εἴπερ αὐτὸ ἐν ἑαυτῷ ἐστίν. ἐν γὰρ ἑνὶ ὂν καὶ ἐκ τούτου μὴ μεταβαῖνον ἐν τῷ αὐτῷ ἂν εἴη, ἐν ἑαυτῷ. Ἔστι γάρ. Τὸ δέ γε ἐν τῷ αὐτῷ ἀεὶ ὂν ἑστὸς δήπου ἀνάγκη ἀεὶ εἶναι. Πάνυ γε. Τί δέ; τὸ ἐν ἑτέρῳ ἀεὶ ὂν οὐ τὸ ἐναντίον ἀνάγκη μηδέποτ' ἐν τῷ αὐτῷ εἶναι, μηδέποτε δὲ ὂν ἐν τῷ αὐτῷ μηδὲ ἑστάναι, μὴ ἑστὸς δὲ κινεῖσθαι; Οὕτως.

Again (β) ταὐτὸν connotes *good*, θάτερον *evil*.

---

[51] These passages probably refer to Plato notwithstanding Philop. *in Arist. Phys.* ed. Vitelli p. 352, 20 ἔλεγον δὲ οἱ Πυθαγόρειοι τὴν κίνησιν εἶναι ἑτερότητα καὶ ἀνισότητα καὶ τὸ μὴ ὄν.

[52] Arist. *Psych.* Γ 10. 8. 433 b 24 is parallel only in appearance.

For this we have Aristotle's express testimony—

Met. A. 6. 988 a 14 ἔτι δὲ τὴν τοῦ εὖ καὶ τοῦ κακῶς αἰτίαν τοῖς στοιχείοις (*sc.* τὸ ταὐτὸν and θάτερον) ἀπέδωκεν ἑκατέροις ἑκατέραν.

Ibid. Δ. 10. 1075 a 34 ἅπαντα τοῦ φαύλου μεθέξει ἔξω τοῦ ἑνός· τὸ γὰρ κακὸν αὐτὸ θάτερον τῶν στοιχείων.

Ibid. M. 8. 1084 a 34 τὰ μὲν γὰρ ταῖς ἀρχαῖς ἀποδιδόασιν, οἷον κίνησιν στάσιν ἀγαθὸν κακόν, τὰ δ' ἄλλα τοῖς ἀριθμοῖς.

Phys. A. 9. 192 a 14 ἡ δ' ἑτέρα μοῖρα τῆς ἐναντιώσεως πολλάκις ἂν φαντασθείη τῷ πρὸς τὸ κακοποιὸν αὐτῆς ἀτενίζοντι τὴν διάνοιαν οὐδ' εἶναι τὸ παράπαν.

Plato, then, would by no means have shrunk from the conclusions of the *reductio ad absurdum* in *Met. N.* 4. 1091 b 25—1092 a 5.

It was partly, no doubt, the facility afforded by the terms ταὐτὸν and θάτερον for the expression of such secondary meanings (*e.g.* the common euphemism of ἕτερος = κακός), which recommended their adoption as symbols for the primary aspects of Idealism.

(B) With regard to the antithesis ἓν καὶ πολλὰ it may be shown that the limitations imposed by philosophic usage differed at different stages of Plato's development.

i. During the period to which the *Republic* and the *Phaedo* belong, the words are sometimes found in a broadly physical sense to denote—

(a) *the one particular with its many attributes:*

Phileb. 14 C ὅταν τις ἐμὲ φῇ Πρώταρχον, ἕνα γεγονότα φύσει, πολλοὺς εἶναι πάλιν τοὺς ἐμὲ καὶ ἐναντίους ἀλλήλοις, μέγαν καὶ σμικρὸν τιθέμενος καὶ βαρὺν καὶ κοῦφον τὸν αὐτόν, καὶ ἄλλα μυρία.

Cp. the drift of *Rep.* 523 A—524 D, *Phaed.* 102 B—103 A, though the phrase does not actually occur in either passage—

(β) *the one particular with its many parts:*

Parm. 129 C εἰ δ' ἐμὲ ἕν τις ἀποδείξει ὄντα καὶ πολλά, τί θαυμαστόν, λέγων, ὅταν μὲν βούληται πολλὰ ἀποφαίνειν, ὡς ἕτερα μὲν τὰ ἐπὶ δεξιά μού ἐστιν, ἕτερα δὲ τὰ ἐπ' ἀριστερά κ.τ.λ.

Cp. *Rep* 524 D—526 B, *e.g.* 525 A ἅμα γὰρ ταὐτὸν ὡς ἕν τε ὁρῶμεν καὶ ὡς ἄπειρα τὸ πλῆθος, 525 E ἐὰν σὺ κερματίζῃς αὐτό (*sc.* the visible unit), ἐκεῖνοι πολλαπλασιοῦσιν, εὐλαβούμενοι μή ποτε φανῇ τὸ ἓν μὴ ἓν ἀλλὰ πολλὰ μόρια.

But even at this date they were normally confined to a narrower and more directly metaphysical scope, being the ordinary[53] equivalents for—

(γ) *the informing Idea and its informed particulars.*

---

[53] An exceptional usage is that of *Parm.* 129 B ἀλλ' εἰ ὃ ἔστιν ἕν, αὐτὸ τοῦτο πολλὰ ἀποδείξει καὶ αὖ τὰ πολλὰ δὴ ἕν, τοῦτο ἤδη θαυμάσομαι (cp. 129 D οὐ τὸ ἓν πολλὰ οὐδὲ τὰ πολλὰ ἕν), where ἕν and πολλά represent *the Ideas of Unity and Multiplicity.*

So, for example, in the two cardinal rubrics of immature Platonism we read—

Rep. 596 A εἶδος γάρ πού τι ἓν ἕκαστον εἰώθαμεν τίθεσθαι περὶ ἕκαστα τὰ πολλά, οἷς ταὐτὸν ὄνομα ἐπιφέρομεν.

Ibid. 476 A αὐτὸ μὲν ἓν ἕκαστον εἶναι, τῇ δὲ τῶν πράξεων καὶ σωμάτων καὶ ἀλλήλων κοινωνίᾳ πανταχοῦ φανταζόμενα πολλὰ φαίνεσθαι ἕκαστον.

ii. The *Philebus* marks a transition. All these denotations are passed in review (*Phileb.* 14 C—15 C), the first two being summarily dismissed, the last alone retained as suggesting problems worthy of serious discussion. Subsequently, however, an important change of nomenclature is observable. For whereas 15 B drew our attention to the cruces of ἓν καὶ πολλά, the διαίρεσις of 16 C—E is μειζόνως διῃρημένη and embraces the three terms ἕν, πολλά, and ἄπειρα. Again, the ἓν καὶ πολλὰ of 15 B were expressly stated to be the one Idea and its many particulars: but in 16 C—E,—though the application is primarily dialectical, and the terms signify Genus, Species, and Specimens,—it is evident from the sequel that Plato is also thinking of its metaphysical bearings; and to the metaphysician ἓν *denotes henceforward the single supreme Mind,* πολλὰ *the subordinate Ideal series,* ἄπειρα *the indefinite range of particular existence.*

iii. In Plato's later writings the revised terminology has become firmly established. It will be remembered, for instance, that the ἕν, πολλά, and ἄπειρα, educed by Parmenides' πλάνη from Platonic data, stood for Mind, the Ideas, and Particulars. And the same phraseology obtains throughout all the works posterior to the *Philebus* as distinct from those of the preceding period. I do not mean to imply that the doctrine underlying the earlier dialogues ignores the unity of the supreme Idea and the indefinity of particulars[54]; nor do I hold that the teaching of the later dialogues fails to attain a higher conception of the singleness and indivisibility of each several Idea: I merely contend that to the reader of Plato's less mature discourse the terms ἓν καὶ πολλά naturally suggest the one Idea and the many particulars, while to the student of his ἀκριβέστεροι λόγοι they represent the supreme Mind and the Ideal Minds—a new term ἄπειρα being added as a truer description of particulars.

iv. It may be objected that this contention is to some extent invalidated by Aristotelian evidence, which shows that the phrase ἓν ἐπὶ πολλῶν continued

---

[54] In point of fact I cannot find a satisfactory example of ἄπειρα = particulars, nor even of ἕν = the supreme Idea, in the earlier dialogues. The nearest approach to the former seems to be *Rep.* 445 C ἓν μὲν εἶναι εἶδος τῆς ἀρετῆς, ἄπειρα δὲ τῆς κακίας. The latter is of course deducible from the use of the singular number.

to be used in the Platonic school as denoting any given Idea. Closer inspection proves that the passages in which that collocation occurs, *viz*—

Met. A. 9. 990 *b* 7, 13, 991 *a* 2 (= *M.* 4. 1079 *a* 2, 9, 32) and *Z.* 16. 1040 *b* 29,[55]

are directed against certain Idealists—probably followers of Xenokrates ὁ νωθρός[56]—who despite the explicit criticism of the *Parmenides* adhered to the ontology of the *Republic*. Further examples of πολλά in the sense of "particulars" (*e.g. Met. A.* 6. 987 *b* 10, 988 *a* 2, *etc.*) may be due to the same inaccuracy which caused the retention of the term μέθεξις in the place of the more exact μίμησις (*Met. A.* 6. 987 *b* 10, *M.* 4. 1079 *a* 25, *Phys. Δ.* 2. 209 *b* 35).

On the other hand Aristotle commonly identifies the Platonic ἄπειρον with the material cause, and habitually speaks of the Ideas as ἀριθμοί,—a word which we have elsewhere seen applied by Plato himself to their multeity (*Parm. l.c.* page 61): so that the regular Aristotelian terminology may be said to agree with that of the later rather than with that of the earlier dialogues.

If the foregoing exposition be accepted as substantially correct, it will be seen that, in strict metaphysical parlance, ταὐτὸν *embraces the* ἓν καὶ πολλά,

---

[55] The list in the *Index Arist.* 618 *a* 25 is incomplete.

[56] Diog. Laert. iv. 2. 6.

θάτερον the ἄπειρα of later Platonism. The supreme Mind and the Ideal Minds, so far as they do not transgress the limits of their own noetic existence, are termed ταὐτόν; so far as they pass beyond those limits into gnostic phase, they are termed θάτερον. And since the objective and subjective aspects of Idealism were distinguished by the same criterion, it is evident that ταὐτὸν and θάτερον may be regarded as apt symbols for the double operation of Mind.

I would end by anticipating two misconceptions. In the first place *the ἑτερότης of the ἕν does not find expression in the ταὐτότης of the πολλά.* For ἑτερότης always connotes the motion and imperfection of γιγνόμενα, whereas the ταὐτότης of the πολλά—*i.e.* the Ideal series—is endowed with the permanence and perfection of ὄντως ὄντα. When, therefore, the Greek commentators on Aristotle speak of the Ideas as ἕτερα,[57] it follows that they are using the term in its logical rather than its metaphysical acceptation, and are referring to the fact that the Ideas are a series of different and differently constituted[58] entities. But

---

[57] *E.g.* Simplic. *in Arist. Phys.* ed. Diels p. 143, 26 ff., 147, 21 ff. Plotinus, though right in saying οὐχ ἑτέρα τοῦ νοῦ ἑκάστη ἰδέα, ἀλλ' ἑκάστη νοῦς. καὶ ὅλος μὲν ὁ νοῦς τὰ πάντα εἴδη, ἕκαστον δὲ εἶδος νοῦς ἕκαστος (*Enn.* V. ix. 8), commits a fatal blunder when he severs ὁ νοῦς from τὸ ἕν by means of ἡ πρώτη ἑτερότης (*Enn.* V. i. 1)

[58] Ideal Numbers are composed of monads which are αἱ μὲν ἐν ἄλλῳ διάφοροι, αἱ δ' ἐν τῷ αὐτῷ ἀριθμῷ ἀδιάφοροι ἀλλήλαις μόναι (Arist. *Met.* M. 7. 1081 b 35 ff.)

such differences do not entitle them to be described as Platonic ἕτερα (*i.e.* ἕτερα αὐτὰ ἑαυτῶν); at most they warrant the use of the word ἄλλα: cp.

Tim. 52 C, where of the particular phenomenon it is said—ἑτέρου δέ τινος ἀεὶ φέρεται φάντασμα, διὰ ταῦτα ἐν ἑτέρῳ προσήκει τινὶ γίγνεσθαι,—
but of the Ideal kingdom—
ἕως ἄν τι τὸ μὲν ἄλλο ᾖ, τὸ δὲ ἄλλο, οὐδέτερον ἐν οὐδετέρῳ ποτὲ γενόμενον ἐν ἅμα ταὐτὸν καὶ δύο γενήσεσθον.

In the second place *the ἑτερότης of τὸ ἕν is not to be confused with the ἑτερότης of τὰ πολλά*. This is at first sight less obvious. It might have been thought that the demands of Necessity would be satisfied and her law fulfilled, if the Ideas alone passed into the sphere of θάτερον, and left the supreme Mind to that νόησις νοήσεως which it enjoys in Aristotle's conception (*Met.* Λ. 9. 1074 b 33). But that such is not the case appears to me certain from the following considerations:—

(1) Plato teaches that οὐσία is necessarily an alliance of ταὐτὸν with θάτερον. If, therefore, τὸ ἕν acquires the latter element only through the evolution of τὰ πολλά, then Unity owes its existence to the Ideas, not the Ideas to Unity. But we have already concluded that the permanence of the Ideal series depends upon the volition of the supreme Mind. Hence, though prepared to allow that Unity does

not as a matter of fact exist without the Ideas, we must deny that its existence is contingent upon theirs. Rather, the Ideas owe their οὐσία—its ἑτερότης as well as its ταὐτότης—to a self-subsisting Unity.

(2) Again, the Ideas are ὄντα, *i.e.* they possess both ταὐτότης and ἑτερότης. Their ταὐτότης they admittedly derive from Unity. Their ἑτερότης either is or is not derived from the same source. If it is, we are justified in discriminating between the ἑτερότης of τὸ ἕν and the ἑτερότης of τὰ πολλά. If it is not, whence comes it? Certainly not from the mere fact that the Ideas are a plurality: that, as we have seen, makes them ἄλλα but not ἕτερα.

(3) The Ideal Minds stand to the supreme Mind in the relation of πολλά to ἕν. It would seem then that they are to be considered multiples of an original Unit. As such, their ταὐτότης presupposes its ταὐτότης, their ἑτερότης its ἑτερότης. Otherwise they would be neither fractional nor integral powers, but utterly incommensurate quantities.

(4) Plato's own words suggest a ἑτεροίωσις of the cosmic ζῷον as distinct from that of the subordinate ζῷα. In drawing a comparison between the intelligible and sensible universe he declares that the partial Animals embraced by the entire Animal answer to the particular specimens contained in a visible cosmos: *Tim.* 30 C τὰ γὰρ δὴ νοητὰ ζῷα πάντα

ἐκεῖνο ἐν ἑαυτῷ περιλαβὸν ἔχει, καθάπερ ὅδε ὁ κόσμος ἡμᾶς ὅσα τε ἄλλα θρέμματα ξυνέστηκεν ὁρατά.[59] *Parm.* 158 A makes the same point: Μετέχειν δέ γε τοῦ ἑνὸς ἀνάγκη τῷ τε ὅλῳ καὶ τῷ μορίῳ ... Οὕτως. Οὐκοῦν ἕτερα ὄντα τοῦ ἑνὸς μεθέξει τὰ μετέχοντα αὐτοῦ; Πῶς δ' οὔ; That is to say that τὸ ὅλον (= τὸ παντελὲς ζῷον of *Tim.* 31 B) as well as τὰ μόρια (= τὰ ἐν μέρους εἴδει ζῷα of *Tim.* 30 C) passes into the sphere of θάτερον.

Agreeably to this *Phileb.* 30 D represents the Creator as having not only νοῦς but also ψυχή— Οὐκοῦν ἐν μὲν τῇ τοῦ Διὸς ἐρεῖς φύσει βασιλικὴν μὲν ψυχήν, βασιλικὸν δὲ νοῦν ἐγγίγνεσθαι διὰ τὴν τῆς αἰτίας δύναμιν κ.τ.λ. And *Phileb.* 30 A clearly distinguishes this cosmic soul from the souls of its particular creations—ΣΩ. Τὸ παρ' ἡμῖν σῶμα ἆρ' οὐ ψυχὴν φήσομεν ἔχειν; ΠΡΩ. Δῆλον ὅτι φήσομεν. ΣΩ. Πόθεν, ὦ φίλε Πρώταρχε, λαβόν, εἴπερ μὴ τό γε τοῦ παντὸς σῶμα ἔμψυχον ὂν ἐτύγχανε, ταὐτά γε ἔχον τούτῳ καὶ ἔτι πάντῃ καλλίονα; ΠΡΩ. Δῆλον ὡς οὐδαμόθεν ἄλλοθεν, ὦ Σώκρατες.

Finally, we have the problematic assignment of two circles to the mundane soul. Now the circle of the Other (*Tim.* 36 C, 38 C) cannot represent the particular souls of men, horses, etc., since they have

---

[59] To the same effect Arius Didymus in Stob. *Ecl.* I. xii. 2a. ed. Wachsmuth i. p. 136, 10.

special περίοδοι (*Tim.* 42 C, 43 D, 85 A, 87 A, 88 B, 91 E), which are expressly distinguished from those of the universe (*Tim.* 47 B, 90 D). Nor can it denote the Ideal ἔμψυχα: for, so far as these possess νόησις they do not belong to the realm of θάτερον at all, and so far as they lapse into γνῶσις they are represented by particulars. It must, therefore, stand for the lower phase of the cosmic soul as distinguished on the one hand from the Ideas, and on the other from their particulars.

(5) If there be no perception of matter "by the cosmic soul apart from the perceptions of finite souls," we are of course driven to say No to the question of the Platonic Parmenides—

Ἆρ' οὖν οἷός τε αὖ ἔσται ὁ θεὸς τὰ παρ' ἡμῖν γιγνώσκειν αὐτὴν ἐπιστήμην ἔχων ; (*Parm.* 134 C)

Sokrates' awe-struck comment—

Ἀλλὰ μὴ λίαν, ἔφη, θαυμαστὸς ὁ λόγος, εἴ τις τὸν
θεὸν ἀποστερήσειε τοῦ εἰδέναι. (*Ibid.* 134 E)—

prepares us, however, to find that in Plato's maturest judgment this decision is reversed, or at any rate evaded. And *Laws* 905 D—

ὅτι μὲν γὰρ θεοί τ' εἰσὶ καὶ ἀνθρώπων ἐπιμελ-
οῦνται, ἔγωγε οὐ παντάπασι φαύλως ἂν φαίην
ἡμῖν ἀποδεδεῖχθαι.—

repeats the assurance of *Phaedo* 62 D—

εὐλόγως ἔχει τὸ θεόν τε εἶναι τὸν ἐπιμελούμενον[60] ἡμῶν καὶ ἡμᾶς ἐκείνου κτήματα εἶναι.

The moral bearings of this question call for further consideration: for the present I proceed, noting merely that if the supreme ζῷον can pay separate attention to the individual souls of men, it must—unless the argumentation of Parmenides be entirely groundless —pass from the ταὐτότης of pure thought into the ἑτερότης of knowledge, opinion, and even sensation. To challenge that passage is indeed to obscure the connection between Plato's ethical speculations and their ontological basis.

(6) Mr. Archer-Hind commenting on *Tim.* 86 E writes:—"Absolute being, absolute *thought*, and absolute goodness are one and the same. Therefore from the absolute or universal *soul* can come no evil." Had he in lieu of "soul" repeated the word "thought," no exception could have been taken to the dictum. As it stands, the second clause seems to me a specific denial of the evil world-soul described in the tenth book of the *Laws*. The description there given cannot be ignored;—

ψυχὴ ... νοῦν μὲν προσλαβοῦσα ἀεὶ θεὸν θεὸς οὖσα, ὀρθὰ καὶ εὐδαίμονα παιδαγωγεῖ πάντα, ἀνοίᾳ δὲ ξυγγενομένη πάντα αὖ τἀναντία τούτοις ἀπεργάζεται. (897 B)—

---

[60] Cp. *Phaedr.* 246 E Ζεὺς διακοσμῶν πάντα καὶ ἐπιμελούμενος.

and it forces upon us the conclusion that the cosmic soul *quâ* cosmic functions not only in the mode of ταὐτὸν as perfect thought, but also in the mode of θάτερον as imperfect thought.

These are the main arguments which tend to show that *the ἑτερότης of the One must not be confused either with the ταὐτότης or with the ἑτερότης of the Many.* Its more precise determination will be attempted in the succeeding section.

§ III. *Theology.*

In discussing the evolution of νοῦς we have more than once had occasion to use the words θεὸς and θεῖος. We are not, however, entitled to adapt theological terms to the purposes of philosophy unless we can return an affirmative answer to the vexed question—Did Plato, or did he not, bring his religious convictions into any intimate connection with his metaphysical views? Dr. Zeller, who here as elsewhere represents modern orthodoxy at its best, holds that theology does not rank with Dialectics, Physics, and Ethics, as a definite part of the Platonic doctrine; that it cannot even be classified under any of these sciences[61]; that, in short, "the particular notions which bring Plato in contact with positive religion are

---

[61] *Plato and The Older Academy*, p. 494.

for the most part mere outworks of his system, or else an inconsistent relapse into the language of ordinary opinion."[62] And yet there are certain *a priori* considerations which militate strongly against the orthodox position. It is difficult to believe that a speculator so thorough-going and fearless as Plato would have shrunk from the attempt to base his own religion on a sound intellectual foundation. And that foundation lay ready to hand. For it must be observed that, if by a personal being is meant one conscious of uniting in itself a diversity of its own states, then the supreme Mind and the Ideal Minds have substantial claims to personality; and further, that in the said Minds is vested the directorate of the universe. We shall not then be sinning against antecedent likelihood, if we enquire how far Plato provides material for the expression of the Idealist creed in terms of divinity.

(A) Broadly speaking we may say that, in the Platonic scheme, the objective realm of ταὐτόν is characterised as divine, and its denizens as deities:

Polit. 269 D τὸ κατὰ ταὐτὰ καὶ ὡσαύτως ἔχειν ἀεὶ καὶ ταὐτὸν εἶναι τοῖς πάντων θειοτάτοις προσήκει μόνοις.

In fact, νόησις and θειότης are everywhere mutual implicates:

---

[62] *Plato and The Older Academy*, p. 505.

Laws 897 B ψυχὴ νοῦν μὲν προσλαβοῦσα ἀεὶ θεὸν θεὸς οὖσα κ.τ.λ.

Phaedr 247 D θεοῦ διάνοια νῷ τε καὶ ἐπιστήμῃ ἀκηράτῳ τρεφομένη.

And this applies on the one hand (*a*) to the supreme Mind, and on the other (*b*) to the Ideal Minds.

(*a*) With regard to the supreme Mind, we have already seen that the functions which the *Philebus* assigns to it are in the *Timaeus* given to ὁ θεός. The phrase τὸν ἀληθινὸν ἅμα καὶ θεῖον νοῦν (*Phileb*. 22 C) and the attribution of this νοῦς βασιλικὸς to *Zeus* (*Phileb*. 30 D) serve to link the two titles together. There is, therefore, no room for doubt that in Plato's teaching—as in that of his immediate successors—absolute Mind and absolute Godhead coincide. Stobaeus, following Aetios, registers the Platonic view correctly in the words ὁ δὲ θεὸς νοῦς ἐστι τοῦ κόσμου.[63]

(*b*) With regard to the Ideas we have the evidence of *Tim*. 37 C—

ὡς δὲ κινηθὲν αὐτὸ καὶ ζῶν ἐνόησε τῶν ἀιδίων θεῶν γεγονὸς ἄγαλμα ὁ γεννήσας πατήρ, ἠγάσθη,—

---

[63] Stob. *Ecl*. I. x. 16 *a* ed. Wachsmuth i. p. 127, 20. *Ecl*. I. i. 29 *b* (Aetios) *ibid*. p. 37, 4 Πλάτων δὲ τὸ ἕν, τὸ μονοφυές, τὸ μοναδικόν, τὸ ὄντως ὄν, τἀγαθόν. Πάντα δὲ τὰ τοιαῦτα τῶν ὀνομάτων εἰς τὸν νοῦν σπεύδει. Νοῦς οὖν ὁ θεός. Cp. *Ecl*. I. vi. 1*a* (Menander) *ibid.* p. 83, 20, I. i. 24, *ibid*. p. 31, 5 τί ποτ' ἐστὶ θεός; νοῦς.

where they are termed θεοὶ as being the first pluralisation[64] of θεός, and ἀίδιοι θεοὶ as being the first pluralisation of that which is an ἀίδιον ζῷον (*Tim.* 37 D). Mr. Archer-Hind well urges[65] that Plato "used this strange phrase with some deliberate purpose in view." I cannot however agree with him that "the significance of so calling them is very hard to see." It appears to me a direct indication that the Ideas are the partial Minds into which the universal Mind multiplies itself.

The *Politicus* perhaps allegorizes the same Unity and Plurality of gods, when it states (271 D *seq.*) that in the golden age the universe as a whole was managed by a θεὸς ἄρχων, its separate portions by θεοὶ ἄρχοντες.[66] These departmental gods are spoken of in terms that certainly suggest Plato's deification of the natural kinds:

τὰ ζῷα κατὰ γένη καὶ ἀγέλας οἷον νομεῖς θεῖοι διειλήφεσαν δαίμονες, αὐτάρκης εἰς πάντα ἕκαστος ἑκάστοις ὢν οἷς αὐτὸς ἔνεμεν. (271 D)

(B) But ταὐτὸν must of necessity pass into θάτερον. There is need, therefore, to examine the subjective manifestation of these objective deities. And since

---

[64] πρῶτα διακεκριμένα τῆς ἀμερίστου ἐνώσεως, as Simplicius *in Arist. Psych.* ed. Hayduck p. 28, 22 calls them.

[65] Ed. *Timaeus* p. 118 *n*.

[66] Cp. *Polit.* 272 E οἱ κατὰ τοὺς τόπους συνάρχοντες τῷ μεγίστῳ δαίμονι θεοί.

we have distinguished the ἑτεροίωσις of the cosmic θεὸς from that of the partial θεοί, our enquiry subdivides itself into two questions: (a) What is the minor mode of the supreme θεός? and (b) What is the minor mode of the Ideal θεοί?

(a) It was shown in the course of the last section that the ἑτερότης of τὸ ἕν is bodied forth as a περιέχων κόσμος, which embraces all particular animals, taking cognisance of their individual conduct, and being in some sort responsible for their special deficiencies. Now the said κόσμος, considered as the visible entire of τὸ ἕν, is of course a unity. Whether we hail from the Academy or the Lyceum, we are bound to recognise ἕνα οὐρανόν[67], because—apart from all question of Idealism—any physical totality may be logically regarded as a single phenomenon.[68] But to infer that "in this case we have an idea with only one particular corresponding" seems to me premature. When Plato mentions the externality of the supreme θεὸς in the singular number, it behoves us to ask first whether it is not this collective unity that is intended. In *Tim.* 34 A—B, for example,—

οὗτος δὴ πᾶς ὄντος ἀεὶ λογισμὸς θεοῦ περὶ τὸν ποτὲ ἐσόμενον θεὸν λογισθεὶς ... τέλεον ἐκ τελέων σωμάτων σῶμα ἐποίησε.—

---

[67] *Tim.* 31 A, cp. Bonitz *Ind. Arist.* p. 542 a 8.

[68] Cp. *Parm.* 164 D ὄγκοι ἔσονται, εἷς ἕκαστος φαινόμενος, ὢν δὲ οὔ. *Soph.* 237 D ἀνάγκη τόν τι λέγοντα ἕν γέ τι λέγειν.

I take it that ὁ ὢν ἀεὶ θεὸς is contrasted with ὁ ποτὲ ἐσόμενος θεός, i.e. God quà eternal with God quà temporal. Again, in *Tim.* 92 C—

ζῷον ὁρατὸν τὰ ὁρατὰ περιέχον, εἰκὼν τοῦ ποιητοῦ, θεὸς αἰσθητός . . . εἷς οὐρανὸς ὅδε μονογενὴς ὤν.—

and in *Tim.* 68 E—

ταῦτα δὴ...ὁ τοῦ καλλίστου τε καὶ ἀρίστου δημιουργὸς ἐν τοῖς γιγνομένοις παρελάμβανεν, ἡνίκα τὸν αὐτάρκη τε καὶ τὸν τελεώτατον θεὸν ἐγέννα.—

God *quà* Creator is opposed to God *quà* created. But we must not on the strength of such passages argue that the supreme being appears to sense-perception as a unitary god. And this for the excellent reason that such an appearance would impugn the very nature of particular existence. To explain. By a particular is meant a localisation of any given νοητὸν ζῷον by itself or any other νοητὸν ζῷον. The percipient Animal and the percept Animal, both functioning in the fourth plane of consciousness, provide what the *Theaetetus* calls κινήσεως δύο εἴδη, πλήθει μὲν ἄπειρον ἑκάτερον, δύναμιν δὲ τὸ μὲν ποιεῖν ἔχον, τὸ δὲ πάσχειν. (156 A). This being so, a unique particular is a contradiction in terms; inasmuch as the predicate "unique" implies that the object is perceived not in its shifting phase of κίνησις but in its permanent condition of στάσις, that is, not as a particular but as an Idea. Hence in every case *particularity connotes numerical indefinity*. The denial of a solitary specimen is confirmed alike by the wording of Parmenides' fourth hypothesis—

Parm. 158 B Τὰ δ' ἕτερα τοῦ ἑνὸς πολλά που ἂν εἴη... Ἐπεὶ δέ γε πλείω ἑνός ἐστι τά τε τοῦ ἑνὸς μορίου καὶ τὰ τοῦ ἑνὸς ὅλου μετέχοντα, οὐκ ἀνάγκη ἤδη πλήθει ἄπειρα εἶναι αὐτά γε ἐκεῖνα τὰ μεταλαμβάνοντα τοῦ ἑνός ;—

and by the testimony of Aristotle:

Met. Z. 15. 1040 a 25 ἔσται γὰρ ἰδέα τις ἦν ἀδύνατον ἐπὶ πλειόνων κατηγορῆσαι ἢ ἑνός. οὐ δοκεῖ δέ, ἀλλὰ πᾶσα ἰδέα εἶναι μεθεκτή.

It would seem, therefore, that the minor mode of the supreme θεὸς may indeed be regarded as a unity, inasmuch as it is a physical totality[69] containing within itself all the visible manifestations of the Ideal θεοί,—

Tim. 30 D ζῷον ἓν ὁρατόν, πάνθ' ὅσα αὑτοῦ κατὰ φύσιν ξυγγενῆ ζῷα ἐντὸς ἔχον ἑαυτοῦ.—

but that nevertheless this περιέχων κόσμος must in some sense be an indefinite plurality, if it represents the ἑτερότης of τὸ ἕν.

And here we should avoid the error of supposing that the particular specimens of the natural kinds

---

[69] Compare Cicero's description of Xenokrates' theology: "Deos enim octo esse dicit; quinque eos qui in stellis vagis nominantur, *unum qui ex omnibus sideribus quae infixa caelo sunt ex dispersis quasi membris simplex sit putandus Deus*, septimum solem adiungit, octavamque lunam." (*De Nat. Deor.* i. 13. 34).

supply the needed plurality. That would be to mistake the ἑτερότης of τὰ πολλὰ for the ἑτερότης of τὸ ἕν.

The whole visible universe is the full concourse of objective θεοί as viewed subjectively by any one of their company localised on the plane of αἴσθησις. But what we are seeking is the single sovereign θεός as viewed by the same spectator on the same plane.

If, then, the θεός Man functioning on the fourth level apprehends the θεός Palm as a multiplicity of palm-trees, there is no reason why he should not similarly apprehend the supreme θεός as a multiplicity of supreme θεοί. Only, whereas particulars are designated by the plural form of the name affixed to their corresponding Idea, and whereas each of the Ideal θεοί has some distinguishing name—Man, Horse, or Palm—from which such a plural may be derived, the supreme θεός has no appellation of the sort. He might, however, as a θεός supreme over the Ideal θεοί, be fittingly titled θεὸς θεῶν, *the God of gods*. Indeed he is so named by Proklos in his account of Platonic Theology:

The. Plat. ii. 11. p. 110 (ὁ πρῶτος θεός) ὡς θεός ἐστι θεῶν[70] ἁπάντων, καὶ ὡς ἑνὰς ἑνάδων,...ἅγιος ἐν ἁγίοις, τοῖς νοητοῖς ἐναποκεκρυμμένος θεοῖς.

---

[70] Cp. the fragment from Porphyry περὶ ἀγαλμάτων cited by Stob. *Ecl.* I. i. 25 ed. Wachsmuth i. p. 31, 8—Ζεὺς οὖν ὁ πᾶς κόσμος, ζῷον ἐκ ζῴων καὶ θεὸς ἐκ θεῶν. Ζεὺς δὲ καὶ < ὁ θεός >, καθὸ νοῦς ἀφ' οὗ προφέρεται πάντα, ὅτι δημιουργεῖ τοῖς νοήμασιν.

When, therefore, we meet the phrase θεοὶ θεῶν we are tempted to find in it the plural (representing the subjective indefinity) of him who is the θεὸς θεῶν. So far as the phrase itself is concerned, this would be a perfectly simple and straightforward solution. But it remains to be seen whether the nature and functions of the θεοὶ θεῶν, as described in the *Timaeus*, tally with those of the supreme νοητὸν ζῷον conceived as the percept of particular percipients.

And first as to their nature. *Tim.* 34 B *seqq.* narrates how the original blend of ψυχή was compounded of the three primal elements. It was used for the cosmic soul, being divided into the circles of the Same and the Other. *Tim.* 41 D tells how the second blend of ψυχή was compounded of the same elements, though in a less pure condition. It went to form the subordinate souls, each of which possessed a similar pair of circles. Now in between these two brews we have the planets described as δεσμοῖς ἐμψύχοις σώματα δεθέντα ζῷα (38 E), and the fixed stars called ζῷα θεῖα καὶ ἀΐδια (40 B). Whence—it may be asked—came the animation of these ζῷα? It could not be furnished by the second mixture of ψυχή, since that had not yet been compounded. Moreover, the first mixture had been entirely used up (36 B) in the making of the cosmic soul. It is obvious, therefore, that the starry ζῷα *are* the externalisation of the cosmic soul as distinguished from the subordinate souls.

It was natural that their bodies should be placed not only in the circle of the Other to perform the planetary functions, but also in the circle of the Same to be a veritable κόσμος. For they are the exponents of the Godhead in the sight of men; and by setting forth the twofold aspect of "their great original" act as an everlasting witness to an eternal truth. It was no mere access of astronomical ardour which led Plato to write:

τῶν νῦν λόγων περὶ τοῦ παντὸς λεγομένων οὐδεὶς ἄν ποτε ἐρρήθη μήτε ἄστρα μήτε ἥλιον μήτε οὐρανὸν ἰδόντων (*Tim.* 47 A).

There can, then, be little doubt that the θεοὶ θεῶν, whom *Tim.* 41 A identifies with these stars, are simply a subjective pluralisation of the supreme Mind. Were we capable of pure νόησις, we should apprehend them as a single θεὸς θεῶν.

The same lesson may be learnt from the *Laws* along with sundry practical corollaries. For it is more than probable that the gods, whose care over men is there vindicated by the Athenian, are identical with the θεοὶ θεῶν of the *Timaeus*. This becomes evident, ὅταν τεκμήρια λέγωμεν ὡς εἰσὶ θεοί, ταῦτα αὐτὰ προφέροντες, ἥλιόν τε καὶ σελήνην καὶ ἄστρα καὶ γῆν ὡς θεοὺς[71] καὶ θεῖα ὄντα (*Laws* 886 D).

---

[71] Cp. *Laws* 950 D ἥλιον...καὶ τοὺς ἄλλους θεούς, 828 C τῶν χθονίων καὶ ὅσους αὖ θεοὺς οὐρανίους ἐπονομαστέον, *Crat.* 397 C φαίνονταί μοι οἱ

And in the conclusion drawn by 899 B I discern a hint that this synod of λαμπροὶ δυνάσται is but the embodiment of a single Mind:

ἄστρων δὲ δὴ πέρι πάντων καὶ σελήνης ἐνιαυτῶν τε καὶ μηνῶν καὶ πασῶν ὡρῶν πέρι τίνα ἄλλον λόγον ἐροῦμεν ἢ τὸν αὐτὸν τοῦτον, ὡς ἐπειδὴ ψυχὴ μὲν ἢ ψυχαὶ πάντων τούτων αἴτιαι ἐφάνησαν, ἀγαθαὶ δὲ πᾶσαν ἀρετήν, θεοὺς αὐτὰς εἶναι φήσομεν, εἴτε ἐν σώμασιν ἐνοῦσαι, ζῷα ὄντα, κοσμοῦσι πάντα οὐρανὸν εἴτε ὅπῃ τε καὶ ὅπως;

It is interesting to note that, as in this passage ψυχὴ and ψυχαὶ are used alternatively, so in those parts of the *Timaeus* which deal with the doings of the θεοὶ θεῶν there is a constant oscillation between the use of the singular and the plural number. Thus we have θεοί (44 D)...θεοῦ (44 E)...θεοί (45 A)...θεός (46 C) ...θεός (47 A)...θεόν (47 B)...θεοῦ (47 C)...θεῶν (47 C). The alternation may be seen on an extended scale from *Tim.* 69 C to almost the end of the dialogue. In 92 A the grammatical change is not even marked, the subject of ἐγέννησαν viz. θεοὶ being supplied from the previous θεοῦ βάσεις ὑποτιθέντος. A still more striking case occurs in 71 A where an actual anacoluthon is

---

πρῶτοι τῶν ἀνθρώπων τῶν περὶ τὴν Ἑλλάδα τούτους μόνους τοὺς θεοὺς ἡγεῖσθαι, οὕσπερ νῦν πολλοὶ τῶν βαρβάρων, ἥλιον καὶ σελήνην καὶ γῆν καὶ ἄστρα καὶ οὐρανόν.

produced: εἰδότες δὲ αὐτό...θεὸς...ξυνέστησε[72]. In much the same way ὁ δημιουργὸς of *Tim.* 28 A, 29 A, *etc.* is pluralised into οἱ δημιουργοὶ of 75 B, ὁ ξυνιστὰς of 29 E into οἱ ξυσστήσαντες of 71 D.

Again, Plato's later writings consistently denote the possession of ταυτότης by the term ἀθάνατον, that of ἑτερότης by the term θνητόν. If, then, the θεοὶ θεῶν were objectively existent as a plurality, they would doubtless be endowed with ἀθανασία. But in *Tim.* 41 B we read:

ἀθάνατοι μὲν οὐκ ἐστὲ[73] οὐδ' ἄλυτοι τὸ πάμπαν, οὔ τι μὲν δὴ λυθήσεσθέ γε οὐδὲ τεύξεσθε θανάτου μοίρας, τῆς ἐμῆς βουλήσεως μείζονος ἔτι δεσμοῦ καὶ κυριωτέρου λαχόντες ἐκείνων, οἷς ὅτ' ἐγίγνεσθε ξυνεδεῖσθε.—

and this agrees with the tenor of *Politicus* 270 A, where the visible cosmos is spoken of as λαμβάνοντα

---

[72] The converse change from singular to plural occurs in *Parm.* 134 D Οὐκοῦν εἰ παρὰ τῷ θεῷ αὕτη ἐστὶν ἡ ἀκριβεστάτη ἐπιστήμη, οὔτ' ἂν ἡ δεσποτεία ἡ ἐκείνων ἡμῶν ποτὲ ἂν δεσπόσειεν, οὔτ' ἂν ἡ ἐπιστήμη ἡμᾶς γνοίη . οὔτε γιγνώσκουσι τὰ ἀνθρώπεια πράγματα θεοὶ ὄντες.

[73] It follows that in *Tim* 69 C πᾶν τόδε ξυνεστήσατο, ζῷον ἓν ζῷα ἔχον τὰ πάντα ἐν αὑτῷ θνητὰ ἀθάνατά τε, and in *Tim.* 92 C θνητὰ γὰρ καὶ ἀθάνατα ζῷα λαβὼν καὶ ξυμπληρωθεὶς ὅδε ὁ κόσμος κ.τ.λ. the "immortal animals" are not—as has commonly been supposed—the stars. Rather, ἀθάνατα ζῷα = *the supreme Mind and the Ideal Minds so far as they are* ταὐτόν, θνητὰ ζῷα = *the supreme Mind and the Ideal Minds so far as they become* θάτερον. Cp. Arist. *Top.* Z. 10. 148 a 15 ὡς Πλάτων ὁρίζεται τὸ θνητὸν προσάπτων ἐν τοῖς τῶν ζῴων ὁρισμοῖς· ἡ γὰρ ἰδέα οὐκ ἔσται θνητή, οἷον αὐτοάνθρωπος.

ἀθανασίαν ἐπισκευαστὴν[74] παρὰ τοῦ δημιουργοῦ. These passages confirm us in the belief that the existence of the starry gods as a plurality is merely subjective and phenomenal.

In brief, the θεοὶ θεῶν are related to the supreme θεός as particulars to their corresponding Idea. Aetios' account of that relation in *Ecl.* I. xii. 1 *a* ed. Wachsmuth i. p. 134, 9—

Ἰδέα ἐστὶν οὐσία ἀσώματος ... πατρὸς ἐπέχουσα τοῖς αἰσθητοῖς τάξιν—

is apparently founded on, and certainly justified by, *Tim.* 50 D where the Idea is compared to a πατήρ, the particular to an ἔκγονον. Now in 42 E the θεοὶ θεῶν with reference to the supreme θεός are called οἱ παῖδες τοῦ πατρός. Similarly in 37 C the latter is ὁ γεννήσας πατήρ,[75] and in 69 C the former are τὰ ἑαυτοῦ γεννήματα.[76] This coincidence of nomenclature, by establishing the proportion—As particulars : their Ideas :: the θεοὶ θεῶν : the supreme θεός—certainly favours the view I have put forward, that *the θεοὶ θεῶν are not an objective but a subjective pluralisation of their Creator.*[77]

---

[74] Cp *Polit.* 273 E θεὸς ὁ κοσμήσας.... ἀθάνατον αὐτὸν καὶ ἀγήρων ἀπεργάζεται·

[75] Cp. *Polit.* 273 B.

[76] *Soph.* 266 B has θεοῦ γεννήματα of particular men *etc.*

[77] Chalcidius *in Tim.* 41 A ed. Wrobel p. 200 well remarks: "Illi enim optimates, id est stellae, non sunt intellegibiles sed sensiles; at vero fabricator eorum intellegibilis adprime."

To deal next with their functions. (1) In *Tim.* 41–42 the θεὸς addresses himself to the θεοὶ θεῶν and says: "Three mortal tribes have still to be created that the universe may be complete. So far as their souls are imperishable and divine, they are mine to make: yours be it to fashion their bodies and thereby cause such part of their souls' activity as is necessarily perishable."

Here Plato distinguishes the direct creations of the θεὸς from the indirect creations of the θεοὶ θεῶν. To the former belongs the task of providing the immortal and passionless self:

Tim. 41 C καθ' ὅσον ... αὐτῶν ἀθανάτοις ὁμώνυμον εἶναι προσήκει, θεῖον λεγόμενον ἡγεμονοῦν τε ... σπείρας καὶ ὑπαρξάμενος.

Ibid. 42 E ἀθάνατον ἀρχὴν θνητοῦ ζώου = 69 C ἀρχὴν ψυχῆς ἀθάνατον—

to the latter that of adding the mortal body and its attendant passions:

Tim. 42 D τὸ δὲ μετὰ τὸν σπόρον τοῖς νέοις παρέδωκε θεοῖς σώματα πλάττειν[78] θνητά, τό τε ἐπίλοιπον, ὅσον ἔτι ἦν ψυχῆς ἀνθρωπίνης δέον προσγενέσθαι, τοῦτο καὶ πάνθ' ὅσα ἀκόλουθα ἐκείνοις ἀπεργασαμένους ἄρχειν.

---

[78] It may be remarked that the office which *Rep.* 415 A (ἀλλ' ὁ θεὸς πλάττων, ὅσοι μὲν ὑμῶν ἱκανοὶ ἄρχειν, χρυσὸν ἐν τῇ γενέσει ξυνέμιξεν, cp. Arist. *Pol.* B. 5. 1264 b 12 ὁ παρὰ τοῦ θεοῦ χρυσός) assigns to the θεὸς is in the *Timaeus* assigned to the θεοὶ θεῶν.

Ibid. 69 C τὸ μετὰ τοῦτο θνητὸν σῶμα αὐτῇ περιετόρνευσαν .... ἄλλο τε εἶδος ἐν αὐτῷ ψυχῆς προσῳκοδόμουν τὸ θνητόν, δεινὰ καὶ ἀναγκαῖα ἐν ἑαυτῷ παθήματα ἔχον.

This, as I understand it, means: men's very selves are due to the evolution of the absolute Mind on the first or noetic plane, being brought about by objective pluralisation; men's bodies and bodily affections are due to the evolution of the absolute Mind on the remaining or gnostic planes, being brought about by subjective pluralisation.

This statement of the case involves one issue of peculiar importance. If the ultimate consciousness of every individual is a direct creation of the Artificer, or—to drop metaphor—an objective multiple of Mind, and if the objective multiples of Mind are none other than the Ideal series, it follows that the souls of particular men, so far as they may be called truly existent, are not to be distinguished from the Idea of Man. The realisation of this truth throws light upon several details of the present passage. We can now see why the ἀθάνατος ἀρχὴ θνητοῦ ζώου was called θεῖον ἡγεμονοῦν τε (*Tim.* 41 C): plainly because it is the Idea, and as dwelling within the pale of ταυτότης is entitled not only to ἀθανασία but also to θειότης. Again, when the Creator urges that, were he to make the perishable part of his creatures, their mortal would put on immortality and take rank with the gods,—

Tim. 41 C δι' ἐμοῦ δὲ ταῦτα γενόμενα καὶ βίου μετασχόντα θεοῖς ἰσάζοιτ' ἄν—
he virtually declares that the distinction between θάτερον and ταὐτὸν would be abolished; transient particulars would invade the dominion of Ideal θεοί.[79]

But if it be conceded that the immortal part of us all is identical with the Idea of Man, which Idea as it appears in the cosmos becomes subjectively attached to bodies and split into a seeming multitude of souls —περὶ τὰ σώματα γιγνομένη μεριστή (*Tim.* 35 A),— there are yet two possible errors which should be signalised.

On the one hand, it must be observed that this procedure in no wise imperils the unity of the Idea; since the multiplicity of particular souls belongs only *potentially* to the realm of Ideal οὐσία. As νοῦς, the Idea is a single eternal Mind. As ἐπιστήμη or δόξα or αἴσθησις, it passes into the manifold activities of human thought. But the latter phase is dynamically latent in the former; the former is the implicit verity of the latter:

Soph. 247 D λέγω δὴ τὸ καὶ ὁποιανοῦν κεκτημένον δύναμιν εἴτ' εἰς τὸ ποιεῖν ... εἴτ' εἰς τὸ πάσχειν ... πᾶν τοῦτο ὄντως εἶναι· τίθεμαι γὰρ ὅρον ὁρίζειν τὰ ὄντα, ὡς ἔστιν οὐκ ἄλλο τι πλὴν δύναμις.

---

[79] This passage then furnishes a parallel to the use of θεοί = "Ideas" in *Tim.* 37 C: cp. also the terminology of the neo-Platonists (p. 112 *n*).

On the other hand, the ancient landmark between the soul and the body of any given individual remains unmoved. Sokrates is a special localisation of the Idea of Man functioning in the mode of lower mentality. As such he is a double being, comprising both soul and body. His soul is the Ideal Animal conceived as *actively cognisant* on the planes of γένεσις: his body—or, to speak strictly, his bodily shape—is the same Animal conceived as *passively cognised* on the same planes.[80] The one, inasmuch as its activity is the procession of an Ideal Mind, Plato regards as the handiwork of God *quâ* Being, *viz.* the supreme θεός.[81] The other, inasmuch as its passivity is the result of imperfect apprehension, he refers to the workmanship of God *quâ* becoming, *viz* the θεοὶ θεῶν.

It may here be objected—and the objection is a valid one—that, allowing the body and its accompanying emotions to be the outcome of imperfect apprehension, we have as yet shown no reason why the θεοὶ θεῶν rather than the lower phase of any other νοητόν ζῷον should be named as the cause of their appearance. The reason, I think, lies in the fact that the Ideal ζῷα are multiples of the supreme ζῷον, whose

---

[80] This doctrine was a refinement upon the teaching of the earlier dialogues, *e.g.* *Phaedrus* 245 E πᾶν γὰρ σῶμα ᾧ μὲν ἔξωθεν τὸ κινεῖσθαι, ἄψυχον, ᾧ δὲ ἔνδοθεν αὐτῷ ἐξ αὑτοῦ, ἔμψυχον, ὡς ταύτης οὔσης φύσεως ψυχῆς.

[81] Cp. *Tim.* 69 C τῶν μὲν θείων αὐτὸς γίγνεται δημιουργός.

subjectivity therefore takes logical precedence of theirs. Plato in fact goes more to the root of the matter by assigning the causation of the θνητὸν γένος to the lower aspect of the supreme θεός. Elsewhere he penetrates beyond their ulterior to their ultimate source.

Tim 41 A Θεοὶ θεῶν, ὧν ἐγὼ δημιουργὸς πατήρ τε ἔργων.

Soph. 265 C ζῷα δὴ πάντα θνητὰ καὶ φυτὰ...μῶν ἄλλου τινὸς ἢ θεοῦ δημιουργοῦντος φήσομεν ὕστερον γίγνεσθαι πρότερον οὐκ ὄντα;

(2) A second office attributed to the θεοὶ θεῶν in *Tim.* 41 D—42 E may be thus expressed. The Artificer begins his task of providing the θεῖον ἡγεμονοῦν τε portion of individuals by dividing the whole mass of soul at his disposal into ψυχὰς ἰσαρίθμους τοῖς ἄστροις. Bearing in mind what was said concerning ψυχὴ μεριστὴ we shall expect Dr. Zeller's view [82] to prove correct, *viz.* that these ψυχαὶ are the souls of particular men. But the point may be certified by a consideration of the word ἰσάριθμοι, whose significance has, I believe, been unduly neglected.

The employment of the terms ὅλον and μόρια to denote the supreme ζῷον and the Ideal ζῷα shows that, in Plato's view, the sum total of the latter represents the content of the former. Now this equivalence was

---

[82] *Plato and The Older Academy* p. 390, n. 8.

not confined to the higher phase of Ideal ταὐτότης: it applied also to the lower order of particular ἑτερότης. Hence the Platonic Parmenides, after stating (*Parm.* 144 C) that οὐσία is split into πλεῖστα μέρη, corrects himself and observes:

Οὐκ ἄρ' ἀληθῆ ἄρτι ἐλέγομεν, λέγοντες ὡς πλεῖστα μέρη ἡ οὐσία νενέμηται, ἀλλ' ἴσα, ὡς ἔοικε, τῷ ἑνί. (144 D—E)

Καὶ μὴν τά γε πάντα μέρη τὰ αὐτοῦ τὸ ἕν ἐστι, καὶ οὔτε τι πλέον οὔτε ἔλαττον ἢ πάντα. (145 C)

From these passages I gather that what Aristotle[83] calls τὰ πολλὰ τῶν συνωνύμων τοῖς εἴδεσιν correspond numerically to the similar phase of τὸ ἕν, that is, to the θεοὶ θεῶν. The meaning of the expression in *Tim.* 41 D will then be as follows. The ψυχαὶ ἰσάριθμοι τοῖς ἄστροις are the souls of men which the Creator divides and distributes to the number of the starry gods, that they may severally learn the laws of the universe. Thus the ψυχαὶ ἰσάριθμοι are particular souls, but *particular souls considered as not yet embodied* and therefore as still the direct handiwork of the Creator. Their state of dynamic multiplicity is of course merely an analytical abstraction; for, if the body be but the soul passively apprehended by lower psychosis, actual multiplicity must synchronise with incarnation. The state of potential plurality is,

---

[83] *Met. A.* 6. 987 *b* 10.

however, recognised and described in *Parm.* 156 D as τὸ ἐξαίφνης[84]—a condition intermediate between οὐσία and γένεσις:

Κατὰ δὴ τὸν αὐτὸν λόγον καὶ ἐξ ἑνὸς ἐπὶ πολλὰ ἰὸν καὶ ἐκ πολλῶν ἐφ' ἓν οὔτε ἕν ἐστιν οὔτε πολλά, οὔτε διακρίνεται οὔτε συγκρίνεται (157 A).

It may be added that the sojourn in the ξύννομος οἴκησις ἄστρου rationalises the influence over a man's character which ancient astrology universally attributed to his birth-star. For the rest, having heard their destiny, these potential particulars are sown into the planets where they are clothed upon with bodies by the subjective action of the late-born gods.

In fine, this examination of the nature and functions of the θεοὶ θεῶν enables us to determine their metaphysical value with some assurance. They are not co-ordinate with the τρία θνητὰ γένη, except in so far as they constitute the ἑτεροίωσις of a νοητὸν ζῷον, but are related to them as the supreme Νοῦς is to the Ideal νοήματα. If the term παράδειγμα be understood to denote the cognitions of ψυχή functioning in the

---

[84] Compare the use of ἐξαίφνης in *Symp.* 210 E ἐξαίφνης κατόψεταί τι θαυμαστὸν τὴν φύσιν καλόν κ.τ.λ., *Gorg.* 523 E αὐτῇ τῇ ψυχῇ αὐτὴν τὴν ψυχὴν θεωροῦντα ἐξαίφνης ἀποθανόντος ἑκάστου. The former passage conceives the individual mind confronting that which is αὐτὸ καθ' αὑτὸ μεθ' αὑτοῦ μονοειδὲς ἀεὶ ὄν, the latter represents the disembodied soul of the particular man after death. Both depict a juxtaposition of the properties of οὐσία and γένεσις, which except in a moment of transition is impossible.

mode of ταὐτόν, and the term εἰκών to denote the cognitions of ψυχὴ functioning in the mode of θάτερον, then I conceive that the position assigned by Plato to the θεοὶ θεῶν may be fairly represented by the following diagram:

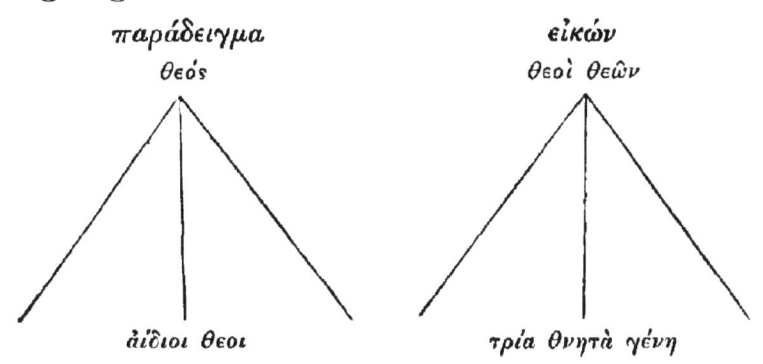

παράδειγμα   εἰκών
θεός   θεοὶ θεῶν

/\   /\

ἀΐδιοι θεοί   τρία θνητὰ γένη

(*b*) Lastly, we approach the question, What of the subjective aspect of the Ideal gods? There is but one fitting term for a minor order of ἀΐδιοι θεοί, namely δαίμονες. And this Plato has used to describe the reasoning powers of particular men:

Tim. 90 A τὸ δὲ περὶ τοῦ κυριωτάτου παρ' ἡμῖν ψυχῆς εἴδους διανοεῖσθαι δεῖ τῇδε, ὡς ἄρα αὐτὸ δαίμονα θεὸς ἑκάστῳ δέδωκε.

Ibid. 90 C ἅτε δὲ ἀεὶ θεραπεύοντα τὸ θεῖον ἔχοντά τε αὐτὸν εὖ κεκοσμημένον τὸν δαίμονα ξύνοικον ἐν αὑτῷ διαφερόντως εὐδαίμονα εἶναι.

By δαίμων then Plato means the intelligence[85]—

---

[85] With the Platonic derivation from δαήμων in *Crat.* 398 B L. and S. compare Archil. 3, 4 ταύτης γὰρ κεῖνοι δαίμονές εἰσι μάχης.

that part of us which is the nearest approximation to Ideal θειότης. It is indeed sometimes[86] called τὸ θεῖον on grounds which we have already examined. But for the most part individuals are relegated to the region of ἑτερότης, and their highest faculty described as—

τὸ θειότατον τῶν παρ' ἡμῖν (*Tim.* 73 A)
τὸ θειότατον τῶν ἐν ἡμῖν (*Ibid.* 88 B)
ὃ θειότατόν τ' ἐστι καὶ τῶν ἐν ἡμῖν πάντων δεσποτοῦν (*Ibid.* 44 D)
τὸ ἑαυτοῦ θειότατον (*Rep.* 589 E).

He who follows its precepts deserves the name of θεῖος (*Rep.* 500 D, *Epist.* ζ'. 340 C), and the resultant life is πάντων τῶν βίων θειότατος (*Phileb.* 33 B, cp. *Laws* 766 A).

Enough has now been said to prove that a theological designation of Plato's Idealism is not chimerical. *The objective aspect of Mind is represented on the one hand by the supreme θεός, and on the other by the Ideal θεοί. The subjective aspect of the former finds expression in the θεοὶ θεῶν; that of the latter in the δαίμονες of individuals.*

If it be asked—In what relation does this hierarchy stand to the evil World-soul of the *Laws*?—I should reply that, since νοῦς is ἀεὶ θεός (*Laws* 897 B), Necessity or the force which produces the degeneration of νοῦς

---

[86] *Tim.* 41 C, 69 D, 72 D.

may be justly described not only as ἄνοια but also as τὸ ἄθεον⁸⁷, whether in the case of the supreme Mind,—

Laws 897 B ψυχὴ...ἀνοίᾳ ξυγγενομένη πάντα αὖ τἀναντία τούτοις ἀπεργάζεται.

Theaet. 176 E παραδειγμάτων, ὦ φίλε, ἐν τῷ ὄντι ἑστώτων, τοῦ μὲν θείου εὐδαιμονεστάτου, τοῦ δὲ ἀθέου ἀθλιωτάτου—

or in that of the subordinate minds,—

Tim. 86 B νόσον μὲν δὴ ψυχῆς ἄνοιαν ξυγχωρητέον.

Rep. 589 E εἰ δὲ τὸ ἑαυτοῦ θειότατον ὑπὸ τῷ ἀθεωτάτῳ τε καὶ μιαρωτάτῳ δουλοῦται...οὐκ ἄρα ἄθλιός ἐστι;

Thus the θεοὶ θεῶν, so far as they represent the θεός, are ἀγαθοὶ πᾶσαν ἀρετήν (*Laws* 899 B), so far as they deviate from his perfection, are evil and responsible for the defects of their dependent creations. Similarly with particular specimens of the natural kinds: so far as they approximate to their Idea, they are θεῖα and εὐδαίμονα; so far as they recede therefrom, they are ἄθεα and κακοδαίμονα.

A word or two may be added with regard to subsequent terminologies. Of Speusippos' usage next to nothing is known; but his severance of νοῦς from ἓν and τἀγαθὸν must have produced theological complications of a serious sort.

---

⁸⁷ Cp. *Tim.* 53 B ὅταν ἀπῇ τινὸς θεός.

With regard to Xenokrates our information is less scanty. Aetios[88] affirms of this philosopher's religious theories that τὰ πρότερα παρὰ τοῦ Πλάτωνος μεταπέφρακεν. And—if we allow for Xenokrates' identification of the Ideas with Mathematical numbers—the statement may be accepted as in the main correct. At least all the gods of the Platonic theocracy play their part in the comprehensive system of Xenokrates. Corresponding to the objective deities we find:

(α) A supreme and unitary Νοῦς called Ζεὺς or ὁ πρῶτος θεός.

(β) Certain θεῶν δυνάμεις or θεῖαι δυνάμεις inherent in elemental forms.

The place of the subjective deities is filled by—

(γ) The stars or Ὀλύμπιοι θεοί, which combine to make a collective οὐρανὸς also known as a θεός. These stars are the result of a union between the One and the indeterminate Dyad or, in allegorical phrase, between Ζεὺς πατήρ and the μήτηρ θεῶν.

(δ) The souls of individual men are called δαίμονες[89], and even the beasts have some instinct of the Divine.[90]

---

[88] Stob. *Ecl.* I. i. 29 *b* ed. Wachsmuth i. p. 37, 2.

[89] Arist. *Top.* B. 6. 112 a 37.

[90] Clemens *Strom.* V. xiii. 87 καθόλου γοῦν τὴν περὶ τοῦ θείου ἔννοιαν Ξενοκράτης . οὐκ ἀπελπίζει καὶ ἐν τοῖς ἀλόγοις ζῴοις (quoted by Zeller *op. cit.* p. 592 *n.*).

Plato's opposition between the power that makes for good and the power that makes for evil reappears perhaps in Xenokrates' broad contrast [91] between Ζεὺς ὕπατος and Ζεὺς νέατος. But the further recognition of ὑποσέληνοι δαίμονες ἀόρατοι seems a mere concession to popular superstition. On the whole, Xenokrates' theology follows the Platonic outlines, though their author's design is marred and obscured by the attempted innovations of his successor.

Aristotle likewise held the truth of the maxim [92]— πάντα φύσει ἔχει τι θεῖον. But a modified system of metaphysics caused certain changes in his theological vocabulary. The conception of a creative νοῦς he appears to have borrowed from Plato's account of the supreme Mind, and, like his master, he describes it by the term θεός:

Met. Λ. 7. 1072 b 18—30. Cp. *frag.* 46, 1483 a 27 ὁ θεὸς ἢ νοῦς ἐστὶν ἢ ἐπέκεινά τι τοῦ νοῦ, *Top. E.* 6. 136 b 7 ζῷον νοητόν = ὁ θεός, *Pol.* Γ. 16. 1287 a 28 ὁ μὲν οὖν τὸν νοῦν κελεύων ἄρχειν δοκεῖ κελεύειν ἄρχειν τὸν θεόν, *Eth. Eud. H.* 12. 1245 b 16 οὐ γὰρ οὕτως ὁ θεὸς εὖ ἔχει, ἀλλὰ βέλτιον ἢ ὥστε ἄλλο τι νοεῖν παρ' αὐτός αὐτόν.

Since, however, Aristotle's ontology recognises no

---

[91] Clemens *Strom.* V. xiv. 116, Plut. *Plat. Qu.* ix. 1, 2. p. 1007 (quoted by R. and P. *Hist. Phil. Gr.* p. 287).

[92] Arist. *Eth. Nic. H.* 14. 1153 b 32.

χωρισταὶ ἰδέαι, he is free to transfer the title θεοὶ from the Ideas to the starry spheres, without the encumbrance of a neologism such as Plato's θεοὶ θεῶν, or the confusion of equivocal names such as those of Xenokrates' gods:

> *Met.* Λ. 8. 1074 *b* 8—14 θεοὺς ... τὰς πρώτας οὐσίας εἶναι, *de mund.* 2. 391 *b* 14—19 θεῶν οἰκητήριον οὐρανὸς ὠνόμασται· κ.τ.λ. Cp. τὰ θεῖα *Psych.* A. 2. 17. 405 *a* 32, *de part. an.* A. 5. 645 *a* 4, ἀνθρώπου πολὺ θειότερα *Eth. Nic.* Z. 7. 1141 *a* 34, τὰ φανερὰ τῶν θείων *Met.* E. 1. 1026 *a* 18, τὰ θειότατα τῶν φανερῶν *Phys.* B. 4. 196 *a* 33, τὰ θεῖα σώματα *Met.* Λ. 8. 1074 *a* 30, *de caelo* B. 12. 292 *b* 32, and the more definite expressions of [Alex.] *in Met.* ed. Hayduck p. 709, 28 ff. θεοὶ ... τοσοῦτοι ὅσαι αἱ σφαῖραι, ἐξηρτημένοι τῆς θειοτάτης καὶ ἀρίστης οὐσίας, *ibid.* p. 709, 33 εἰσὶν οὖν θεοὶ καὶ θεῖον πλῆθος περιέχον τὴν ὅλην φύσιν καὶ τὸν ἄπαντα κόσμον, *ibid.* p. 721, 31 εἷς θεός ἐστι. τὰ γὰρ τῶν πλανωμένων αἴτια θεοὶ μέν, ἀλλὰ μεθέξει καὶ τῷ βουλήματι τοῦ πρώτου καὶ μακαριωτάτου ἐξήρτηνται νοός.

Again, Aristotle—who is similarly impressed with the divine nature of thought (*Psych.* A. 4. 14. 408 *b* 29, *Met.* Λ. 8. 1074 *b* 16, *de part. an.* Δ. 10. 686 *a* 28, *de an. gen.* B. 3. 736 *b* 27)—speaks of particular minds in terms that repeat the language of the Platonic dialogues:

> Eth. Eud. H. 14. 1248 a 27 opposes τὸ ἐν ἡμῖν θεῖον to ἐν τῷ ὅλῳ θεός.
> Eth. Nic. K. 7. 1177 a 16 τῶν ἐν ἡμῖν τὸ θειότατον.
> Probl. ΑΓ. 7. 962 a 22 (cp. 9. 962 a 35) uses τὸ θειότατον τῶν περὶ ἡμᾶς of the human head.

It is, therefore, highly probable that Plato's teaching was the source of the saying attributed to his pupil:

> Clemens Strom. VI. vi. 53 Ἀριστοτέλης δαίμοσι κεχρῆσθαι πάντας ἀνθρώπους λέγει συνομαρτοῦσιν αὐτοῖς παρὰ τὸν χρόνον τῆς ἐνσωματώσεως, προφητικὸν τοῦτο μάθημα λαβὼν καὶ καταθέμενος εἰς τὰ ἑαυτοῦ βιβλία, μὴ ὁμολογήσας ὅθεν ὑφείλετο τὸν λόγον τοῦτον.
> Cic. de fin. ii. 12. 40 "hominem ad duas res, ut ait Aristoteles, ad intellegendum et agendum esse natum quasi *mortalem deum.*"
> Arist. frag. 187, 1511 a 43 τοῦ ... λογικοῦ ζῴου τὸ μέν ἐστι θεός, τὸ δὲ ἄνθρωπος, τὸ δὲ οἷον Πυθαγόρας.

It might be shown that the theology of the neo-Platonists in some measure revived the usage of the Academy. Plotinus, for example, mentions—

> (a) ὁ πατὴρ θεός [93], i.e. the supreme Triad of τὸ ἓν + ὁ νοῦς + ἡ ψυχή.

---

[93] Enn. V. 1. 1.

(β) The νοεραὶ δυνάμεις, i.e. the Platonic Ideas, which consist in the supreme Νοῦς and, as sharing its animation, are termed θεοί [94].

(γ) The ὁρώμενοι θεοί [95], i.e. the stars.

(δ) The δαίμονες and the θεοὶ [96] of particular men.

But to pursue the subject would carry us too far afield. It is of more immediate importance to pass from the theological aspect of Plato's philosophy to the moral deductions which he expressly drew therefrom, bearing in mind that his ontology was from first to last intended to serve as a sound basis for ethical reflection.

---

[94] *Enn.* V. 1 4, cp *ibid.* II. ix 8 πῶς οὐκ ἄν τις ἄγαλμα ἐναργὲς καὶ καλὸν τῶν νοητῶν θεῶν εἴποι, *ibid.* V. 1 7 πᾶν μὲν τὸ τῶν ἰδεῶν κάλλος, πάντας δὲ θεοὺς νοητούς. Iamblichus too calls the Ideas νοεροί (v. l. νοητοί) θεοί ap. Prokl. *in Tim.* 94 C.

[95] *Enn.* V. 1. 4, cp. *ibid.* V. 1 2 ἔστι δὲ καὶ ἥλιος θεός, ὅτι ἔμψυχος, καὶ τὰ ἄλλα ἄστρα.

[96] *Enn.* V. 1 2, 4 Plotinus was himself guided by a θεός, according to Porphyry, others by their respective δαίμονες,—Μακάριος εἰ θεὸν ἔχων τὸν δαίμονα καὶ οὐ τοῦ ὑφειμένου γένους τὸν συνόντα (*Vit. Plot.* § 10)

PART III.

METAPHYSICAL DESCENT AND MORAL ASCENT.

In the foregoing chapter I have emphasised the distinction between the objective and the subjective aspects of Plato's ontology. The former was found to be the purposive pluralisation of a supreme Mind, abiding in eternal self-sameness, and invested with all the credentials of divinity. The latter was the necessary ἔκστασις of every such Mind, whereby it passed out of the sphere of identical being into that of diverse becoming, and stooped from the sovereignty of an Ideal θεός to the subservience of individual δαίμονες. This declension is, however, counterbalanced by certain compensatory tendencies which must not be overlooked. Metaphysics indeed compels a ὅδος κάτω, but Morality with equal insistence demands a ὅδος ἄνω; and it remains to present the dictates of the one in such a manner as will satisfy the claims of the other.

Now it will be remembered that we have repeatedly described the objective world as a pattern, the subjective world as its copy. And this language applies not only to particulars themselves which, whether they be the θεοὶ θεῶν or the τρία θνητὰ γένη, are in any case semblances of higher verities,—

Tim. 39 E τοῦτο δὴ τὸ κατάλοιπον ἀπειργάζετο αὐτοῦ πρὸς τὴν τοῦ παραδείγματος ἀποτυπούμενος φύσιν. ᾗπερ οὖν νοῦς ἐνούσας ἰδέας τῷ ὃ ἔστι ζῷον, οἷαί τε ἔνεισι καὶ ὅσαι, καθορᾷ, τοιαύτας καὶ τοσαύτας διενοήθη δεῖν καὶ τόδε σχεῖν. εἰσὶ δὴ τέτταρες, μία μὲν οὐράνιον θεῶν γένος, ἄλλη δὲ πτηνὸν καὶ ἀεροπόρον, τρίτη δὲ ἔνυδρον εἶδος, πεζὸν δὲ καὶ χερσαῖον τέταρτον—

but also to the conditions of particular existence. For Time, according to Plato, is an image of Eternity, and Space a simulacrum of Ideal Otherness.

The former fact is stated in so many words:

Tim. 37 D εἰκὼ δ' ἐπινοεῖ κινητόν τινα αἰῶνος ποιῆσαι, καὶ διακοσμῶν ἅμα οὐρανὸν ποιεῖ μένοντος αἰῶνος ἐν ἑνὶ κατ' ἀριθμὸν ἰοῦσαν αἰώνιον εἰκόνα, τοῦτον ὃν δὴ χρόνον ὠνομάκαμεν.

The latter is a legitimate inference from *Tim* 52 C, where the thesis that we wrongly import spacial conceptions into the world of Ideas is supported by the following argument:—

" A particular has not an absolute but a relative existence; it is in fact the mere phantasm of another object: hence it demands a something in which it may appear, unless indeed it is to be reduced to an utter nonentity. [This something is Space.] But in the region of real existence for one thing (*sc.* Idea) to be formed in another thing (*sc.* Idea [97]) would be to make that other thing both one and two, which is impossible. [Therefore between the Ideas there is no Space, but only Otherness.]"

This amounts to saying that Space, the medium of subjective pluralisation, corresponds to numerical Otherness, the medium of objective pluralisation. Thus the question raised by Aristotle in *Phys. Δ.* 2. 209 *b* 33—

Πλάτωνι μέντοι λεκτέον . . . διὰ τί οὐκ ἐν τόπῳ τὰ εἴδη καὶ οἱ ἀριθμοί, εἴπερ τὸ μεθεκτικὸν ὁ τόπος, εἴτε τοῦ μεγάλου καὶ τοῦ μικροῦ ὄντος τοῦ μεθεκτικοῦ εἴτε τῆς ὕλης, ὥσπερ ἐν τῷ Τιμαίῳ γέγραφεν—

will be met by the answer that the term τόπος is not rightly used till Ideal alterity has passed into individual extension.

It was this doctrine—that particulars and the modes of particular existence bear to ideas and the modes of Ideal existence the relation of an εἰκών to

---

[97] Mr. Archer-Hind (ed. *Tim.* p. 171) paraphrases:—"For true reason declares that, while the type is one, and the image another, they must be apart; for they cannot exist one in the other and so be one and two at once." But surely τὸ μὲν and τὸ δὲ are both ὄντως ὄντα, *i.e.* Ideas: this is shown by the whole form of construction εἰκόνι μὲν κ.τ.λ. . . . τῷ δὲ ὄντως ὄντι. It is no question of "the old doctrine of παρουσία," but a clear statement of the reason why particulars are extended, Ideas unextended.

its παράδειγμα—which determined the whole allegorical form of the *Timaeus*, and so popularised the belief that "This visible World is but a Picture of the invisible, wherein, as in a Pourtraict, things are not truely, but in equivocal shapes, and as they counterfeit some more real substance in that invisible fabrick." The peculiar value of this imagery is that it links the world of relative to the world of absolute being, and thereby expresses just that aspect of Idealism which might best serve as a basis for the structure of morality. In other words, the artistic setting of the *Timaeus* has a special significance of its own, inasmuch as the *raison d'être* of Plato's ethics may be said to lie in the simple reflection that, if the world as we know it is a portrait, it ought to be as exact a portrait as possible.

Starting from this point of contact between Metaphysics and Morals, I shall attempt to show how the larger lines of matured Platonism mark out the rational end of individual conduct. In so doing we should remember that the true unit of voluntary action is not the particular but the νοητὸν ζῷον. Nevertheless ἀνθρώποις διαλεγόμεθα, ἀλλ' οὐ θεοῖς, and therefore—

> "We must translate our motives, like our speech,
> Into the lower phrase that suits the sense
> O' the limitedly apprehensive. Let
> Each level have its language!"

It will be convenient to begin by resuming the

constitution of the moral agent. Every νοητὸν ζῷον possesses four faculties, namely νοῦς, ἐπιστήμη, δόξα, αἴσθησις,—the three last being moments in the subjective evolution of the first, and opposed to it as γένεσις to ὄντως οὐσία. Particulars which, as such, belong to the region of γιγνόμενα are consequently debarred from νόησις: they are, however, endowed with ἐπιστήμη, δόξα, and αἴσθησις [98], though in the lower forms of life even these are to a greater or less extent in abeyance

This catalogue of the cognitive powers accords well with the usage of the more advanced Platonic writings. In the earlier dialogues pure thought is not unfrequently ascribed to individual thinkers (e.g. Rep. 511 C, D, 524 C, Phaed. 83 B. alib.) The Philebus adopts a half-way position; for it expressly distinguishes the human νοῦς of 21 D, 22 C, 58 D, from the ἀληθινὸς καὶ θεῖος νοῦς of 22 C, 28 C, 30 D. But the Timaeus nowhere [99] speaks of the particular man as possessing νοῦς: it describes him as being at most a νοῦ καὶ ἐπιστήμης ἐραστήν (46 D), and his finest faculty as τῶν

---

[98] Cp. Stob. Ecl. I. lxi. 1 (Hermes) ed. Wachsmuth i p. 275, 16 ὁ νοῦς ἐν τῷ θεῷ, ὁ λογισμὸς ἐν τῷ ἀνθρώπῳ. Aristotle after describing (Met Λ. 9 1074 b 35 seqq.) the νόησις νοήσεως of the supreme Being continues φαίνεται δ᾽ ἀεὶ ἄλλου ἡ ἐπιστήμη καὶ ἡ αἴσθησις καὶ ἡ δόξα καὶ ἡ διάνοια, ἑαυτῆς δ᾽ ἐν παρέργῳ.

[99] It does indeed use the phrase νοῦν ἔχειν (68 B), νοῦν ἔχων (89 B) = "sensible, reasonable," and the compounds ἐννοεῖν (87 D), κατανοεῖν (90 D) etc. But to avoid them would have been mere pedantry.

διανοημάτων ἡ ἐκ τοῦ νοῦ φερομένη δύναμις [100] (71 B). To females and the lower animals it alludes in 91 D—92 B, arranging them in a descending scale according as they approximate to or recede from that higher mentality—νοῦ καὶ ἀνοίας ἀποβολῇ καὶ κτήσει (92 B); while 77 B brings even vegetable life into the same register,—ᾧ δόξης μὲν καὶ λογισμοῦ (= ἐπιστήμης) τε καὶ νοῦ μέτεστι τὸ μηδέν, αἰσθήσεως [101] δέ. In like manner the second hypothesis of the *Parmenides* enumerates the powers of the human intellect:

Parm. 155 D καὶ ἐπιστήμη δὴ εἴη ἂν αὐτοῦ καὶ δόξα καὶ αἴσθησις, εἴπερ καὶ νῦν ἡμεῖς περὶ αὐτοῦ πάντα ταῦτα πράττομεν—

but, as we have seen sometime since, this dialogue confines the range of pure thought to the Ideal world.

Here, however, we encounter a difficulty which has beset the student of the Platonic system ever since *Parm.* 134 B was penned. If the realm of true existence is μόνῳ θεατὴ νῷ (*Phaedr.* 247 C), and if νοῦς

---

[100] This strange expression seems chosen to escape the direct attribution of νοῦς to a particular. Similarly in 51 D, where Plato calls the Ideas ἀναίσθητα ὑφ' ἡμῶν εἴδη, νοούμενα μόνον, the position of the pronoun is instructive.

[101] Simplicius (*in Arist. Psych.* ed. Hayduck p. 317, 11) states that plants ἔχειν μέν τινα αἴσθησιν, ἀμυδροτέραν δὲ ἢ κατὰ τὰ ἄλλως ζῶντα, καὶ ὡς ἔφη Πλάτων οἷον καθεύδουσαν αἴσθησιν. Similarly Empedokles (according to Sextus *Math.* viii. 286) πάντα ἠξίου λογικὰ τυγχάνειν, καὶ οὐ ζῷα μόνον ἀλλὰ καὶ φυτά, ῥητῶς γράφων· πάντα γὰρ ἴσθι φρόνησιν ἔχειν καὶ νώματος αἶσαν.

is not allowed to the individual as such, how is it that Plato himself feels so secure about his ground-plan of a supreme Mind existent both as a unity and as a plurality? The confidence which he displays e.g. in—

Tim. 29 B τοῦ μὲν οὖν μονίμου καὶ βεβαίου καὶ μετὰ νοῦ καταφανοῦς μονίμους καὶ ἀμεταπτώτους, καθ' ὅσον [οἷόν] τε ἀνελέγκτοις προσήκει λόγοις εἶναι καὶ ἀκινήτοις, τούτου δεῖ μηδὲν ἐλλείπειν—

could only be justified by the actual intuition of an Ideal θεός:

Tim. 72 D τὰ μὲν οὖν περὶ ψυχῆς ... τὸ μὲν ἀληθὲς ... θεοῖ [102] ξυμφήσαντος, τότ' ἂν οὕτω μόνως διισχυριζοίμεθα· τό γε μὴν εἰκός κ.τ.λ.,

and that intuition is beyond the reach of the individual, however great his genius and however unceasing his efforts. As Chalcidius [103] puts it, "sine divinitatis adminiculo ipsa per se anima nihil valeat spectare atque intellegere divinum."

The difficulty was a real one, and such as to bring a consistent thinker within sight of scepticism:

Parm 135 C τί οὖν ποιήσεις φιλοσοφίας πέρι; ποῖ τρέψει ἀγνοουμένων τούτων;

Plato meets it by two considerations. (1) The highest

---

[102] Cp. *Tim.* 68 D θεὸς μὲν τὰ πολλὰ εἰς ἓν ξυγκεραννύναι καὶ πάλιν ἐξ ἑνὸς εἰς πολλὰ διαλύειν ἱκανῶς ἐπιστάμενος ἅμα καὶ δυνατός, ἀνθρώπων δὲ οὐδεὶς οὐδέτερα τούτων ἱκανὸς οὔτε ἔστι νῦν οὔτ' εἰσαῦθίς ποτ' ἔσται.

[103] *In Plat. Tim.* 41 E, ed. Wrobel p. 202.

human ἐπιστήμη, though it can never attain to divine νόησις, may yet be reckoned an approximation thereto [104]:

Tim. 51 E καί τοῦ μέν (*sc.* δόξης ἀληθοῦς) πάντα ἄνδρα μετέχειν φατέον, νοῦ δὲ θεούς, ἀνθρώπων δὲ γένος βραχύ τι.

The γένος in question is no doubt τὸ τῶν φιλοσοφούντων ὀρθῶς γε καὶ ἀληθῶς γένος (*Epist.* ζ 326 A). Philosophers may in a sense be said νοῦ μετέχειν inasmuch as their intelligence leads them to desiderate certain transcendent fixities in nature as a basis for the ἐπιστήμη which they do possess. They apprehend τὰν μὲν ἰδέαν νόῳ κατ' ἐπιστάμαν... τὰ δ' ἀπογεννάματα αἰσθήσι καὶ δόξᾳ (*Tim. Locr.* 94 B). And it is to this ἀγαθῶν ἀνδρῶν ὁμοφράδμων νόησις [105] that Plato appeals when he wishes to establish any fundamental truth. See, for example, the tenor of—

Phileb. 28 C πάντες γὰρ συμφωνοῦσιν οἱ σοφοὶ ... ὡς νοῦς ἐστὶ βασιλεὺς ἡμῖν οὐρανοῦ τε καὶ γῆς.

Nevertheless the wisdom of men is at best only earth-born. It cannot by itself provide the needed "divinitatis adminiculum." Hence Plato, half in jest, half seriously, delights to invest his authorities with a supernatural halo, and to speak of their contributions to knowledge as of a divine revelation. In *Soph.* 216 B

---

[104] See the admirable remarks of Mr. Archer-Hind ed. *Timaeus* pp. 48—49.

[105] Plat. *Epist.* d. 310 A.

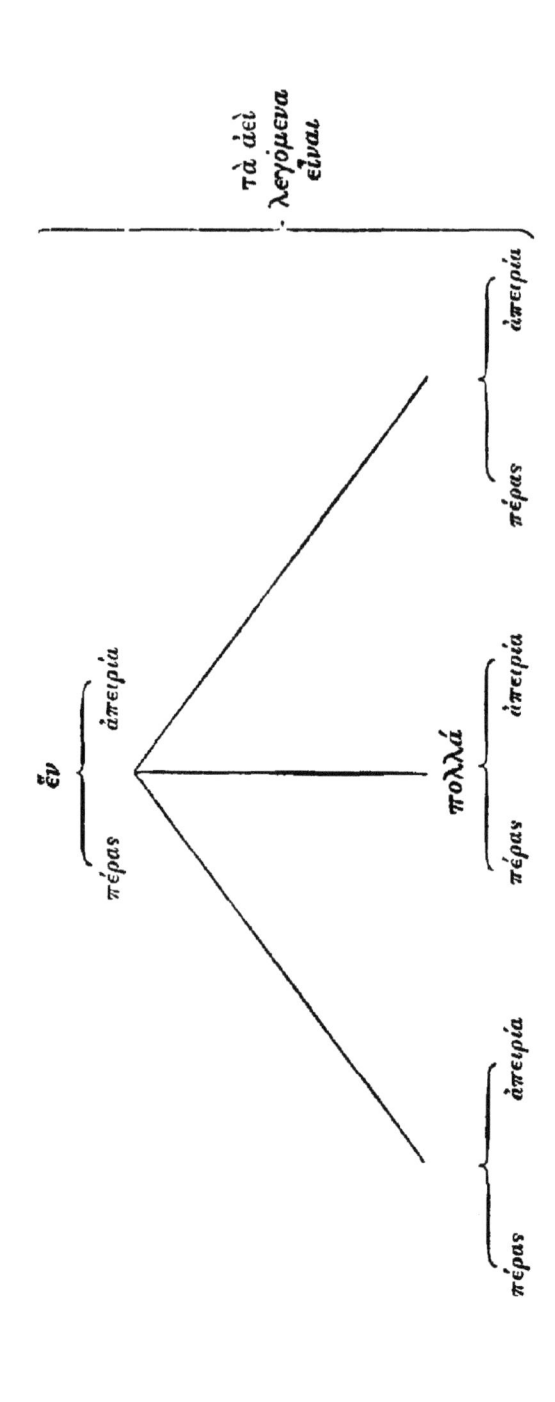

$$
\overbrace{}^{\tau\grave{\alpha}\ \dot{\alpha}\epsilon\grave{\iota}\ \lambda\epsilon\gamma\acute{o}\mu\epsilon\nu\alpha\ \epsilon\tilde{\iota}\nu\alpha\iota}
$$

$\underbrace{\pi\acute{\epsilon}\rho\alpha\varsigma}_{}\underbrace{}_{\tilde{\epsilon}\nu}\underbrace{\dot{\alpha}\pi\epsilon\iota\rho\acute{\iota}\alpha}_{}\qquad\underbrace{\pi\acute{\epsilon}\rho\alpha\varsigma}_{}\underbrace{}_{\pi o\lambda\lambda\acute{\alpha}}\underbrace{\dot{\alpha}\pi\epsilon\iota\rho\acute{\iota}\alpha}_{}\qquad\underbrace{\pi\acute{\epsilon}\rho\alpha\varsigma}_{}\underbrace{}\underbrace{\dot{\alpha}\pi\epsilon\iota\rho\acute{\iota}\alpha}_{}$

the critic of immature Idealism is θεός τις ἐλεγκτικός; and in *Phileb.* 16 C the revised ontology is called in so many words "a gift of the gods to mankind"—

> θεῶν μὲν εἰς ἀνθρώπους δόσις, ὥς γε καταφαίνεται ἐμοί, ποθὲν ἐκ θεῶν ἐρρίφη διά τινος Προμηθέως ἅμα φανοτάτῳ τινὶ πυρί· καὶ οἱ μὲν παλαιοί, κρείττονες ἡμῶν καὶ ἐγγυτέρω θεῶν οἰκοῦντες, ταύτην φήμην παρέδοσαν, ὡς ἐξ ἑνὸς μὲν καὶ ἐκ πολλῶν ὄντων τῶν ἀεὶ λεγομένων εἶναι, πέρας δὲ καὶ ἀπειρίαν ἐν αὑτοῖς ξύμφυτον ἐχόντων.

The last phrase of this passage aptly expresses just that scheme which one particular man could not by his unaided reason have descried; it gives us the appended diagram, in which ἕν denotes the supreme Mind, and πολλά the Ideal series.

(2) But if any one turns a deaf ear to this theory of inspiration, or quotes by way of retort *Rep.* 381 E—

> μηδ' αὖ ὑπὸ τούτων ἀναπειθόμεναι αἱ μητέρες τὰ παιδία ἐκδειματούντων, λέγουσαι τοὺς μύθους κακῶς, ὡς ἄρα θεοί τινες περιέρχονται νύκτωρ πολλοῖς ξένοις καὶ παντοδαποῖς ἰνδαλλόμενοι, ἵνα μὴ ἅμα μὲν εἰς θεοὺς βλασφημῶσιν, ἅμα δὲ τοὺς παῖδας ἀπεργάζωνται δειλοτέρους—

Plato can fall back on a less pregnable position. He holds that the souls of individuals have before their incarnation stood face to face with the Creator, and learnt from his lips τὴν τοῦ πάντος φύσιν (*Tim.* 41 E). This they were enabled to do, because the souls of men conceived as not yet associated with their bodies do not differ from the Idea of Man, under whose intuition all noetic existence would naturally fall.[106] The doctrine of Anamnesis is in fact the safeguard of Idealism. It may be denied: but it can hardly be disproved, and—as has before been hinted—it presupposes some such relation of the ideas to Mind as was elicited from the assumptions of the *Parmenides*.

The confinement of pure thought to the world of Ideas cannot, then, invalidate the foundations of the Idealist system, because the individual philosopher not only builds upon the experience of previous thinkers but also possesses an innate criterion of his own structure:

Phaedrus 249 B, C δεῖ γὰρ ἄνθρωπον ξυνιέναι κατ' εἶδος λεγόμενον, ἐκ πολλῶν ἰὸν αἰσθήσεων εἰς ἓν λογισμῷ ξυναιρούμενον. τοῦτο δέ ἐστιν ἀνάμνησις ἐκείνων, ἅ ποτ' εἶδεν ἡμῶν ἡ ψυχὴ συμπορευθεῖσα θεῷ καὶ ὑπεριδοῦσα ἃ νῦν εἶναί φαμεν καὶ ἀνακύψασα εἰς τὸ ὂν ὄντως. διὸ δὴ δικαίως μόνη πτεροῦται ἡ τοῦ φιλοσόφου διάνοια· πρὸς γὰρ ἐκείνοις ἀεί ἐστι μνήμῃ κατὰ δύναμιν, πρὸς οἷσπερ θεὸς ὢν θεῖός ἐστι.

---

[106] Diog. Laert. iii. 38 ἰδιαίτατα μὲν σοφίαν ἡγεῖται (*sc.* Plato) εἶναι τὴν τῶν νοητῶν καὶ ὄντως ὄντων ἐπιστήμην, ἥν φησι περὶ θεὸν καὶ ψυχὴν σώματος κεχωρισμένην.

The removal of this difficulty in epistemology also clears the way for ethical advance. It might have been argued that to make the world as we know it conform to an Ideal pattern is a futile task for those who have no acquaintance with that pattern. But if it be conceded that we can not only approach to such knowledge but also appraise our own progress, the reduction of individual conduct to directive rules demands immediate attention.

The foremost of these rules, as laid down by Plato, is the general obligation of ὁμοίωσις θεῷ. This was indeed a duty inculcated at all stages of his philosophic development, with the constant qualification of approximate success

Rep. 500 C θείῳ δὴ καὶ κοσμίῳ ὅ γε φιλόσοφος ὁμιλῶν κόσμιός τε καὶ θεῖος εἰς τὸ δυνατὸν ἀνθρώπῳ γίγνεται.

Ibid. 613 B ἐπιτηδεύων ἀρετὴν εἰς ὅσον δυνατὸν ἀνθρώπῳ ὁμοιοῦσθαι θεῷ.

Phaedrus 253 A εὐποροῦσι διὰ τὸ συντόνως ἠναγκάσθαι πρὸς τὸν θεὸν βλέπειν, καὶ ἐφαπτόμενοι αὐτοῦ τῇ μνήμῃ, ἐνθουσιῶντες, ἐξ ἐκείνου λαμβάνουσι τὰ ἔθη καὶ τὰ ἐπιτηδεύματα, καθ' ὅσον δυνατὸν θεοῦ ἀνθρώπῳ μετασχεῖν (cp. 249 C).

Theaet. 176 A, B διὸ καὶ πειρᾶσθαι χρὴ ἐνθένδε ἐκεῖσε φεύγειν ὅ τι τάχιστα. φυγὴ δὲ ὁμοίωσις θεῷ κατὰ τὸ δυνατόν.

Tim. 29 E πάντα ὅ τι μάλιστα γενέσθαι ἐβουλήθη παραπλήσια ἑαυτῷ.

Laws 716 C τὸν οὖν τῷ τοιούτῳ (*sc.* θεῷ) προσφιλῆ γενησόμενον εἰς δύναμιν ὅ τι μάλιστα καὶ αὐτὸν τοιοῦτον ἀναγκαῖον γίγνεσθαι.

But with the modification of the earlier metaphysic it became possible to employ more precise definition. I have said that in Plato's maturer view the individual man consists of soul and body—soul being the active, body the passive function of the same entity. One result of this is that the later dialogues, while determining the human τέλος in a twofold application, emphasise the complementary nature of both its aspects. The *Timaeus*, for example, affirms that οὐδεμία ξυμμετρία καὶ ἀμετρία μείζων ἢ ψυχῆς αὐτῆς πρὸς σῶμα αὐτό (87 D), and insists on parallel development as a mutual security. And the *Laws*, adopting the customary division of παίδευσις into Music and Gymnastic, interpret the former to mean τὰ τῆς φωνῆς μέχρι τῆς ψυχῆς πρὸς ἀρετῆς παιδείαν, the latter τὰ μέχρι τῆς τοῦ σώματος ἀρετῆς (673 A).

(A) To speak first of ψυχή. The rational end for individual souls is not—as we might have supposed—the minimising of the difference between their own ἐπιστήμη and the νόησις of their corresponding Idea. For the Ideas themselves are—as Aristotle says (*Met.* M. 6. 1080 *b* 12, *alib.*)—Numbers involving τὸ πρότερον καὶ ὕστερον, that is, a definite succession of

Minds, each of which exhibits some part of the entire Mind and takes rank according to its noetic ποσόν. Hence Plato finds the *summum bonum* in conformity to the supreme θεός rather than in resemblance to any of the Ideal θεοί.

But how is this ὁμοίωσις θεῷ to be effected? Particulars, as such, are debarred from rising to the spaceless and timeless condition of pure thought. Happily for us, the supreme θεός no less than the Ideal θεοὶ passes into space and time as a plurality possessed of ἐπιστήμη, δόξα, αἴσθησις. *The aim and object of particular morality is approximation to the supreme θεός as revealed to us in the θεοὶ θεῶν.* Our ἐπιστήμη, our δόξα, our αἴσθησις, must be made like to theirs. Otherwise we shall have failed of life's true purpose:

Tim. 90 D τῷ δ' ἐν ἡμῖν θείῳ ξυγγενεῖς εἰσὶ κινήσεις αἱ τοῦ παντὸς διανοήσεις καὶ περιφοραί· ταύταις δὴ ξυνεπόμενον ἕκαστον δεῖ τὰς περὶ τὴν γένεσιν ἐν τῇ κεφαλῇ διεφθαρμένας ἡμῶν περιόδους ἐξορθοῦντα διὰ τὸ καταμανθάνειν τὰς τοῦ παντὸς ἁρμονίας τε καὶ περιφορὰς τῷ κατανοουμένῳ τὸ κατανοοῦν ἐξομοιῶσαι κατὰ τὴν ἀρχαίαν φύσιν, ὁμοιώσαντα δὲ τέλος ἔχειν τοῦ προτεθέντος ἀνθρώποις ὑπὸ θεῶν ἀρίστου βίου πρός τε τὸν παρόντα καὶ τὸν ἔπειτα[107] χρόνον.

---

[107] These last words are noteworthy. Had the *bonum* been defined as approximation to any single Idea, it might have been inapplicable to

This statement supersedes all previous and partial determinations. It is introduced by words which epitomise the teaching of the *Republic*, the clause—

θεραπεία δὲ δὴ παντί (*sc.* τῆς ψυχῆς εἴδει) πάντως μία, τὰς οἰκείας ἑκάστῳ τροφὰς καὶ κινήσεις ἀποδιδόναι (90 C)—

recognising just that apportioned activity which is the mark of genuine justice.[108] Nor do we lose sight of the μικτὸς βίος advocated in the *Philebus*, for with this conception of the rational object is closely linked a σκέψις ἀνθρωπίνης εὐδαιμονίας καὶ ἀθλιότητος (*Theaet.* 175 C). As in the *Republic* εὐδαιμονία was proportioned to attainment of δικαιοσύνη (*Rep.* 580 B, C), so in the later dialogues true pleasure depends upon the realisation of the human end :[109]

Theaet. 176 E παραδειγμάτων ... ἐν τῷ ὄντι ἑστώτων, τοῦ μὲν θείου εὐδαιμονεστάτου, τοῦ δὲ ἀθέου ἀθλιωτάτου.

Laws 664 B τὸν αὐτὸν ἥδιστόν τε καὶ ἄριστον ὑπὸ θεῶν βίον λέγεσθαι φάσκοντες ἀληθέστατα ἐροῦμεν.

the particulars of that Idea *in their future life*, because such particulars may by metempsychosis change their status in the Ideal order.

[108] Cp. *e.g. Rep.* 433 E ἡ τοῦ οἰκείου τε καὶ ἑαυτοῦ ἕξις τε καὶ πρᾶξις δικαιοσύνη ἂν ὁμολογοῖτο, 441 D Μνημονευτέον ἄρα ἡμῖν, ὅτι καὶ ἡμῶν ἕκαστος, ὅτου ἂν τὰ αὑτοῦ ἕκαστον τῶν ἐν αὐτῷ πράττῃ, οὗτος δίκαιός τε ἔσται καὶ τὰ αὑτοῦ πράττων.

[109] Diog. Laert. iii. 42 περὶ δὲ ἀγαθῶν ἢ κακῶν τοιαῦτα ἔλεγε (*sc.* Plato)· τέλος μὲν εἶναι τὴν ἐξομοίωσιν τῷ θεῷ· τὴν δ' ἀρετὴν αὐτάρκη μὲν εἶναι πρὸς εὐδαιμονίαν κ.τ.λ.

Ibid. 732 E δεῖ δὴ τὸν κάλλιστον βίον ἐπαινεῖν μὴ μόνον ὅτι τῷ σχήματι κρατεῖ πρὸς εὐδοξίαν, ἀλλὰ καὶ ὡς ... κρατεῖ καὶ τούτῳ ὃ πάντες ζητοῦμεν, τῷ χαίρειν πλείω, ἐλάττω δὲ λυπεῖσθαι παρὰ τὸν βίον ἅπαντα.

The external manifestation of the supreme Mind is called collectively a εὐδαίμων θεός (*Tim.* 34 B). The philosopher who studies truth κτήσεως ἕνεκα εὐδαίμονος βίου, καθ' ὅσον ἡμῶν ἡ φύσις ἐνδέχεται (*Tim.* 68 E) may win much felicity in the present life—

Tim. 90 C ἅτε δὲ ἀεὶ θεραπεύοντα τὸ θεῖον ἔχοντά τε αὐτὸν εὖ κεκοσμημένον τὸν δαίμονα ξύνοικον ἐν αὑτῷ διαφερόντως εὐδαίμονα εἶναι—

and in the future—

Ibid. 42 B πάλιν εἰς τὴν τοῦ ξυννόμου πορευθεὶς οἴκησιν[110] ἄστρου, βίον εὐδαίμονα καὶ συνήθη ἕξοι.

For in truth the συναγυρμὸς φρονήσεως, the conversion of opinion into knowledge, is μυρίῳ πρὸς εὐδαιμονίαν διαφέρων (*Politic.* 272 C). Even on the perceptive plane conformity to nature's design is attended by pleasure. Thus of sensation in general we read:

Tim. 64 C τὸ μὲν παρὰ φύσιν ... ἀλγεινόν, τὸ δ' εἰς φύσιν ... ἡδύ.

---

[110] The number of the θεοὶ θεῶν must balance that of the τρία θνητὰ γένη (see p. 103). Hence the philosopher is said to travel to the οἴκησις of the star, not to become an actual star himself.

Tim. 81 D—E κατὰ φύσιν μεθ' ἡδονῆς ἐξέπτατο. πᾶν γὰρ τὸ μὲν παρὰ φύσιν ἀλγεινόν, τὸ δ' ᾗ πέφυκε γιγνόμενον ἡδύ.

Ibid. 83 A τάξιν τῶν κατὰ φύσιν οὐκέτ' ἴσχοντα περιόδων, ἐχθρὰ μὲν αὐτὰ αὑτοῖς διὰ τὸ μηδεμίαν ἀπόλαυσιν ἑαυτῶν ἔχειν—

and of the single senses:

Taste.—*Tim.* 66 B ὁπόταν ἡ ξύστασις ... οἰκεία τῇ τῆς γλώττης ἕξει πεφυκυῖα ... ἡδὺ καὶ προσφιλὲς παντὶ πᾶν τὸ τοιοῦτον.

Smell.—*Ibid.* 67 A τό θ' ἡδὺ καὶ τὸ λυπηρὸν ... τὸ μὲν ... βιαζόμενον ... τὸ δὲ ... πάλιν ᾗ πέφυκεν ἀγαπητῶς ἀποδιδόν.

Hearing.—*Ibid.* 80 B ἡδονὴν μὲν τοῖς ἄφροσιν, εὐφροσύνην δὲ τοῖς ἔμφροσι διὰ τὴν τῆς θείας ἁρμονίας μίμησιν ἐν θνηταῖς γενομένην φοραῖς παρέσχον.

In the last extract ἡδονή is the emotion normally accompanying that which conforms to nature; εὐφροσύνη is the higher feeling due to consciousness of that conformity.

(B) Secondly, we have to consider the character and conditions of σῶμα. Here a distinction must be made between matter and shape. The material out of which our limbs are apparently constructed is but a portion of the whole ὑποδοχὴ γενέσεως, borrowed therefrom (*Phileb.* 29 C) and to be returned thereto

(*Tim.* 43 A). By a law of orderly development, akin to that which fixes the quadruple classification of the natural kinds, this ὑποδοχὴ is figured throughout with the forms of the four elements—forms which represent not indeed any αὐτὰ καθ' αὐτά, self-existent Ideas, but still certain αὐτὰ ἐφ' ἑαυτῶν,[111] logically distinct types. In this substrate the transient shapes of particulars, the εἰσιόντα καὶ ἐξιόντα of *Tim.* 50 C, are momentarily expressed. They are declared to be τῶν ὄντων ἀεὶ μιμήματα; for bodily shape is—as already stated—the individual soul as viewed by our imperfect faculties, and the individual soul is but the Idea as it passes into the triple phase of genetic thought. This holds good, whether percipient and percept belong to different species or to the same, or again coincide in a single personality. So far as method is concerned it matters not whether Sokrates beholds a star, or a friend, or himself. In any case a νοητὸν ζῷον is cognised by a νοητὸν ζῷον on the plane of sensation, and the result must be a localisation of the former by the latter in the ὑποδοχή.

Now it is clear enough that the material content of this localisation is a fractional part of the whole cosmic σύστασις. What is not at once clear is the determination of specific contour and its connection with the shape of the universe. Why, for example,

---

[111] *Tim.* 51 B.

is Sokrates' body unlike that of a star, and by no means hard to distinguish from that of his friend? And how are all three related to the mundane sphere?

The answer to these questions, though implicit rather than explicit in Plato's writings, seems inevitable. If a particular shape *is* a particular soul as it appears to particular cognition, it follows that difference of embodiment presupposes difference of soul. In fact we formulate the law: *As is the imitation of the active ψυχή, so will be the imitation of the passive σῶμα.* Individual souls were grouped under certain definite types, *viz.* the νοητὰ ζῶα, according to their degree of approximation to the cosmic soul. Therefore individual bodies will be similarly grouped under certain fixed forms, *viz.* the natural kinds, according to their degree of approximation to the cosmic body. A being endowed with superhuman— say, stellar—thought will be apprehended not as a man but as a star. Again, within the limits of each several species differences of personal shape will be referred to differences of personal attainment, allowance being made for certain retarding tendencies soon to be noticed.

That in Plato's view physical was thus dependent upon psychical development may be gathered from Aristotle's criticism in *Psych.* A. 3. 22–23, 407 b 15–24:
συνάπτουσι γὰρ καὶ τιθέασιν εἰς σῶμα τὴν ψυχήν, οὐθὲν προσδιορίσαντες διὰ τίν' αἰτίαν καὶ πῶς

ἔχοντος τοῦ σώματος. καίτοι δόξειεν ἂν τοῦτ᾽ ἀναγκαῖον εἶναι· διὰ γὰρ τὴν κοινωνίαν τὸ μὲν ποιεῖ τὸ δὲ πάσχει καὶ τὸ μὲν κινεῖται τὸ δὲ κινεῖ, τούτων δ᾽ οὐθὲν ὑπάρχει πρὸς ἄλληλα τοῖς τυχοῦσιν. οἱ δὲ μόνον ἐπιχειροῦσι λέγειν ποῖόν τι ἡ ψυχή, περὶ δὲ τοῦ δεξομένου σώματος οὐθὲν ἔτι προσδιορίζουσιν, ὥσπερ ἐνδεχόμενον κατὰ τοὺς Πυθαγορικοὺς μύθους τὴν τυχοῦσαν ψυχὴν εἰς τὸ τυχὸν ἐνδύεσθαι σῶμα· δοκεῖ γὰρ ἕκαστον ἴδιον ἔχειν εἶδος καὶ μορφήν.

The objection here brought against the *Timaeus*, which admits the κοινωνία of an active soul with a passive body, is that adherents of this theory are satisfied when they have determined the nature of the former and do not trouble themselves about the fitness of the latter. The objection is a typical one. It amounts to a complaint that the theory is inconsistent, not with Plato's presuppositions, but with Aristotle's rejection of them: as is said elsewhere of those who posit Ideal Numbers,—

πρὸς μὲν τὴν ὑπόθεσιν, ὀρθῶς λέγουσιν, ὅλως δ᾽ οὐκ ὀρθῶς· πολλὰ γὰρ ἀναιροῦσιν (*Met.* M. 7. 1082 *b* 32).

From the Platonic standpoint to determine the ποιότης of a given soul was also to determine the ποιότης of its body, inasmuch as that body *is* the visualisation of that soul. This account of the relation subsisting between the two is confirmed by

Tim. 91 D—92 B, a passage which implies throughout that the nature of the body depends upon the nature of the soul. It agrees, too, with the priority always assigned by Plato to ψυχή as analytically contrasted with σῶμα, e.g.

Tim. 34 B, C τὴν δὲ δὴ ψυχὴν οὐχ ὡς νῦν ὑστέραν ἐπιχειροῦμεν λέγειν, οὕτως ἐμηχανήσατο καὶ ὁ θεὸς νεωτέραν· οὐ γὰρ ἂν ἄρχεσθαι πρεσβύτερον ὑπὸ νεωτέρου ξυνέρξας εἴασεν.

Laws 896 B ὀρθῶς ἄρα καὶ κυρίως ἀληθέστατά τε καὶ τελεώτατα εἰρηκότες ἂν εἶμεν ψυχὴν μὲν προτέραν γεγονέναι σώματος ἡμῖν, σῶμα δὲ δεύτερόν τε καὶ ὕστερον ψυχῆς ἀρχούσης ἀρχόμενον κατὰ φύσιν.

Moreover, it justifies certain materialistic descriptions of soul which occur for the most part in the *Timaeus* and are sometimes almost obtrusively unspiritual. In 87 A, for example, it is said of bodily humours that, when τὴν ἀφ' αὑτῶν ἀτμίδα τῇ τῆς ψυχῆς φορᾷ ξυμμίξαντες ἀνακερασθῶσι, παντοδαπὰ νοσήματα ψυχῆς ἐμποιοῦσι. And in 43 D sensations are described as σφοδρῶς σείουσαι τὰς τῆς ψυχῆς περιόδους. So too the bonds that bind soul to body are mentioned in a strangely tangible and visible connection:

τούτοις ξύμπασιν ἀρχὴ μὲν ἡ τοῦ μυελοῦ γένεσις· οἱ γὰρ τοῦ βίου δεσμοὶ τῆς ψυχῆς τῷ σώματι ξυνδουμένης ἐν τούτῳ διαδούμενοι κατερρίζουν τὸ θνητὸν γένος (73 B).

These and similar examples of verbal license Aristotle is never weary of attacking; his motive—if we may trust his followers—being the elimination of all metaphor and inexactitude from the domain of rigid science:

> Simplic. *in Arist. Psych.* ed. Hayduck p. 28, 11
> Ἀριστοτέλης ... ἀεὶ εἰωθὼς ... οὐκ ... ἀναιρεῖν αὐτὴν τὴν ἀλήθειαν, ἀλλὰ μόνον τὴν τῶν ὀνομάτων κατάχρησιν.

Still, when in *Psych.* A. 3. 11, 406 b 25—23, 407 b 26 he refutes at length the manner in which ὁ Τίμαιος φυσιολογεῖ τὴν ψυχὴν κινεῖν τὸ σῶμα, it is hard to acquit him of ignoring the real justification for such language, namely Plato's belief that matter is only another aspect of mind—a belief which warranted the extension of physical terminology to psychical phenomena, and even palliated the chiasmus of the cosmic soul.

There is, however, one difficulty besetting this view of the relation between mind and matter which has not yet been examined. If the body is the soul as apprehended by particular cognition, how can there be any such disproportion between soul and body as is contemplated in *Tim.* 87 D?—

> ψυχὴν ἰσχυρὰν καὶ πάντῃ μεγάλην ἀσθενέστερον καὶ ἔλαττον εἶδος ὅταν ὀχῇ, καὶ ὅταν αὖ τοὐναντίον ξυμπαγῆτον τούτω, οὐ καλὸν ὅλον τὸ ζῷον.

At first sight this passage certainly appears to gainsay the rule enunciated above: "As is the imitation of the active ψυχή, so will be the imitation of the passive σῶμα." But a little reflection will show that the two statements are quite compatible. If a and p denote the active and passive aspects of the individual Sokrates on the plane of ἐπιστήμη, a' and p' the same aspects on the plane of δόξα, a'' and p'' on the plane of αἴσθησις, then the law concerning the parallel development of ψυχή and σῶμα may be represented by a series of equations:—

$$S.$$
$$a = p$$
$$a' = p'$$
$$a'' = p''$$

Suppose now that Sokrates, though intellectually superior to the average man, suffers from some physical defect, say τὸ ἔξω τῶν ὀμμάτων. By the law of correspondence this peculiar conformation of the eyes must accurately express a limitation of the power of sight. But such limitation may well coexist with, or even be brought on by, unusual mental development. Indeed it is just this sacrifice of one set of faculties to another that Plato here deprecates. Let us, he says, have no ill-conditioned disparity between higher and lower functions. If a be fully developed and a'' starved, or if a be starved and a'' fully developed, in either case there is a lack of symmetry about τὸ ξυναμφότερον, ζῶον ὃ καλοῦμεν.

Tim. 88 B μία δὴ σωτηρία πρὸς ἄμφω, μήτε τὴν ψυχὴν ἄνευ σώματος κινεῖν μήτε σῶμα ἄνευ ψυχῆς, ἵνα ἀμυνομένω γίγνησθον ἰσορρόπω καὶ ὑγιῆ.

As a practical precept, both μελέτη διανοίᾳ, the exercise of active thought, and σωμασκία, the cultivation of a healthy frame, are alike enjoined upon one who would imitate the example set by the Universe— the result being a mode of life more harmonious than the high-souled but somewhat ascetic aspirations of the *Phaedo*:

Phaed. 67 D τὸ μελέτημα αὐτὸ τοῦτό ἐστι τῶν φιλο σόφων, λύσις καὶ χωρισμὸς ψυχῆς ἀπὸ σώματος.

Soul and body are indeed distinct, but the distinction is no longer to be an antagonism. Rather it is the contrast between inseparable complements. Active and passive functions are to the particular what νοεῖν and νοεῖσθαι are to the Idea.

Granting, then, that physical condition is determined by psychical development, we return to consider the effect produced upon the one by the graduated attainment of the other.

The nearest approach to the νόησις of the supreme θεός is, we hold, to be found in the sublime intelligence of the θεοὶ θεῶν[112]. Consequently the best imitation of that circularity which symbolises[113] pure thought will be the spherical shapes and revolving orbits of the οὐράνιοι θεοί:

Tim. 40 A τῷ δὲ παντὶ προσεικάζων εὔκυκλον ἐποίει ... κινήσεις δὲ δύο προσῆψεν ἑκάστῳ, τὴν μὲν ἐν ταὐτῷ κατὰ ταὐτὰ περὶ τῶν αὐτῶν ἀεὶ τὰ αὐτὰ ἑαυτῷ διανοουμένῳ, τὴν δὲ εἰς τὸ πρόσθεν.

Aristophanes' myth turns to similar account the οὐλοφυεῖς τύποι of the Empedoklean cosmogony. He makes the children of the sun, the earth, and the moon, still bear the impress of their divine origin:

Symp. 189 E, 190 B ὅλον ἦν ἑκάστου τοῦ ἀνθρώπου τὸ εἶδος στρογγύλον, νῶτον καὶ πλευρὰς κύκλῳ ἔχον ... περιφερῆ δὲ ἦν καὶ αὐτὰ καὶ ἡ πορεία αὐτῶν διὰ τὸ τοῖς γονεῦσιν ὅμοια εἶναι.

As regards the present human frame, the θεοὶ θεῶν have confined the revolutions of immortal soul in a terrestrial body, whereof the cranium is a copy of the cosmos:

Tim. 44 D τὰς μὲν δὴ θείας περιόδους δύο οὔσας τὸ τοῦ παντὸς σχῆμα ἀπομιμησάμενοι περιφερὲς ὂν εἰς σφαιροειδὲς σῶμα ἐνέδησαν, τοῦτο ὃ νῦν κεφαλὴν ἐπονομάζομεν, ὃ θειότατόν τ' ἐστὶ καὶ τῶν ἐν ἡμῖν πάντων δεσποτοῦν.

---

[112] They are repeatedly said to follow the example of the supreme θεός, *e.g. Tim.* 41 C, 42 E, 69 C.

[113] *Tim.* 34 A, *Laws* 898 A.

Tim. 73 C τὴν ... τὸ θεῖον σπέρμα οἷον ἄρουραν μέλλουσαν ἕξειν ἐν αὐτῇ περιφερῆ πανταχῇ πλάσας. The rest of the body is a mere ὑπηρεσία αὐτῷ (*Tim.* 44 D); yet, inasmuch as it contains τὸ λοιπὸν καὶ θνητὸν τῆς ψυχῆς, it was fashioned of the next best shape:

ἅμα στρογγύλα καὶ προμήκη[114] διῃρεῖτο σχήματα (73 D).

This difference in dignity is marked by two curious expressions. The head is held in position by sinews which the Creator περιστήσας κύκλῳ περὶ τὸν τράχηλον ἐκόλλησεν ὁμοιότητι (*Tim.* 75 D): whereas in making the vertebral column he acted τῇ θατέρου προσχρώμενος ... δυνάμει (*ibid.* 74 A). Apart from one another these expressions are barely intelligible. Viewed together, they recall *Tim.* 57 E στάσιν μὲν ἐν ὁμαλότητι, κίνησιν δὲ εἰς ἀνωμαλότητα ἀεὶ τιθῶμεν· αἰτία δὲ ἀνισότης αὖ τῆς ἀνωμάλου φύσεως, where—as I showed from Aristotle—ἀνισότης is equivalent to ἡ θατέρου δύναμις. In short, Plato means that the backbone is flexible, while the head is not.

So strong is his faith in the microcosmic structure of the human body that in *Tim.* 81 A he does not scruple to apply the word οὐρανὸς to it:

τὰ δὲ ἔναιμα ... περιειλημμένα ὥσπερ ὑπ' οὐρανοῦ ξυνεστῶτος ἑκάστου τοῦ ζώου, τὴν τοῦ παντὸς ἀναγκάζεται μιμεῖσθαι φοράν.

---

[114] For πρόμηκες as a deterioration of σφαιροειδὲς cp. *Tim.* 91 E προμήκεις τε καὶ παντοίας ἔσχον τὰς κορυφάς, ὅπῃ συνεθλίφθησαν ὑπὸ ἀργίας ἑκάστων αἱ περιφοραί.

The significance of this phrase will become clearer if we consider that, not only does the vibration of the ὑποδοχὴ correspond to the due motions of the body,—

Tim. 88 C καὶ τὰ μέρη θεραπευτέον, τὸ τοῦ παντὸς ἀπομιμούμενον εἶδος.

Ibid. 88 D ἐὰν δὲ ἥν τε τροφὸν καὶ τιθήνην τοῦ παντὸς προσείπομεν μιμῆταί τις, καὶ τὸ σῶμα μάλιστα μὲν μηδέποτε ἡσυχίαν ἄγειν ἐᾷ, κινῇ δὲ καὶ σεισμοὺς ἀεί τινας ἐμποιῶν αὐτῷ ... κατακοσμῇ, ... κατὰ τὸν πρόσθεν λόγον, ὃν περὶ τοῦ παντὸς ἐλέγομεν, ... ὑγίειαν παρέξει—

but even the concentric spheres of air and fire, which form the mantle of the universe, find their counterpart in the fiery and airy envelopes of the human frame. This, I believe, is the purport of the Platonic theory of respiration, the main points of which may here be summarised.

The passage in which that theory is set forth (*Tim.* 78 A—79 E, cp. *Tim. Locr.* 101 D) has a reputation for difficulty, which it would not, I think, have gained had two facts been borne in mind. To begin with, the whole apparatus of breathing is independent of the animal organism [115]; the ζῷον was already πλασθὲν

---

[115] This is not so puerile a notion as it seems at first sight to be. "We can as yet hardly say what are even the local boundaries that

when the contrivance was added to it (*Tim.* 78 C). And secondly, the preliminary remarks in 78 A show that πάντα ὅσα ἐξ ἐλαττόνων ξυνίσταται στέγει τὰ μείζω, τὰ δ᾽ ἐκ μειζόνων τὰ σμικρότερα οὐ δύναται : hence the structure of the human body is pervious to both air and fire, but fire which is πάντων γενῶν σμικρομερέστατον excludes air.

According to Plato, the Creator constructed a network or bag (πλέγμα ... οἷον οἱ κύρτοι [116]), which was apparently formed of two layers—the outer one (τὸ κύρτος) of air, the inner one of fire. This πλέγμα or κύρτος was subdivided into a couple of smaller bags (ἐγκύρτια) also made of air. The whole, by alternate impletion and depletion, swings to and fro through the

---

divide the organism from its environment. When does the air in our lungs begin to belong to us, and when does it cease to be a constituent of the body?" (Lotze *Microcosmus* i. 136).

[116] By a κύρτος is meant a basket of wicker work with a wide mouth but a comparatively narrow neck, used for catching fish : see the illustrations in Rich *Dict. Ant. s.v.* 'nassa,' Daremberg & Saglio *Dict. Ant. s.v.* 'colum.' Prof. Cook Wilson in his polemic on the *Timaeus* p. 78 *seq.* adopts M. Th. H. Martin's view that the mouth of the trap must have the ends of the reeds pointing inwards. But he himself admits that "there is nothing about such a hindrance in Plato," and it seems more probable that κύρτος here denotes that form of fish-trap which was closed by a lid ; for we should thus obtain a parallel between the lid and the closing of mouth and nostrils. Oppian *Hal.* iii. 341—370 gives a full account of this κύρτος with a lid : when the trap is full, the fisherman claps to the lid and lifts the whole out of the water—ἡνίκα γὰρ πολλοί τε καὶ εὐλιπέες τελέθωσι, | δὴ τότ᾽ ἀνὴρ κύρτοιο περὶ στόμα πῶμα καλύπτει | εὖ ἀραρός· τοὺς δ᾽ ἔνδον ἐν ἕρκεϊ πεπτηῶτας | ὑστάτιον κνώσσοντας ἀνείρυσεν.

body εἰς τὴν ἐκ τῆς κοιλίας ἐπὶ τὰς φλέβας ὑδρείαν. The process may readily be followed by the help of the appended illustration. It comprises two movements, (a) ἐκπνοή and (b) ἀναπνοή. (a) *Expiration*. We start with our ἐγκύρτια full of air (fig. i). This air, heated by the fiery envelope, escapes upwards by the nearest way εἰς τὴν αὐτοῦ χώραν ἔξω πρὸς τὸ ξυγγενές. The nearest way is κατὰ τὸ στόμα καὶ τὰς ῥῖνας. As it issues thence, it would leave a vacuum behind it, did not the principle of περίωσις come into operation. By this principle the whole κύρτος is compressed, so that the air at *A*, which was just outside the body, enters διὰ μανῶν τῶν σαρκῶν and occupies the position *B* described as τὸ τῶν στηθῶν καὶ τοῦ πλεύμονος. (b) *Inspiration*. The air at *B* (fig. ii) is now in its turn heated by the fiery envelope, and rushing out the nearest way—διὸ μανῶν τῶν σαρκῶν—sets up περίωσις again. The περίωσις forces fresh air κατὰ τὸ στόμα καὶ τὰς ῥῖνας into the ἐγκύρτια, and we reach our original position once more.

This arrangement of air and fire in concentric layers recalls the elemental λήξεις of *Tim.* 53 A, 63 B *seqq.*, and the oscillation of the whole is described in terms which tally with the αἰώρα of *Phaed* 111 E:—

Tim. 78 E διαιωρούμενον . . . διὰ τῆς κοιλίας.

Ibid. 80 D τοῦ πυρός, αἰωρουμένῳ . . . ἐντὸς τῷ πνεύματι ξυνεπομένου, τὰς φλέβας τε ἐκ τῆς κοιλίας τῇ ξυναιωρήσει πληροῦντος.

FIG.1

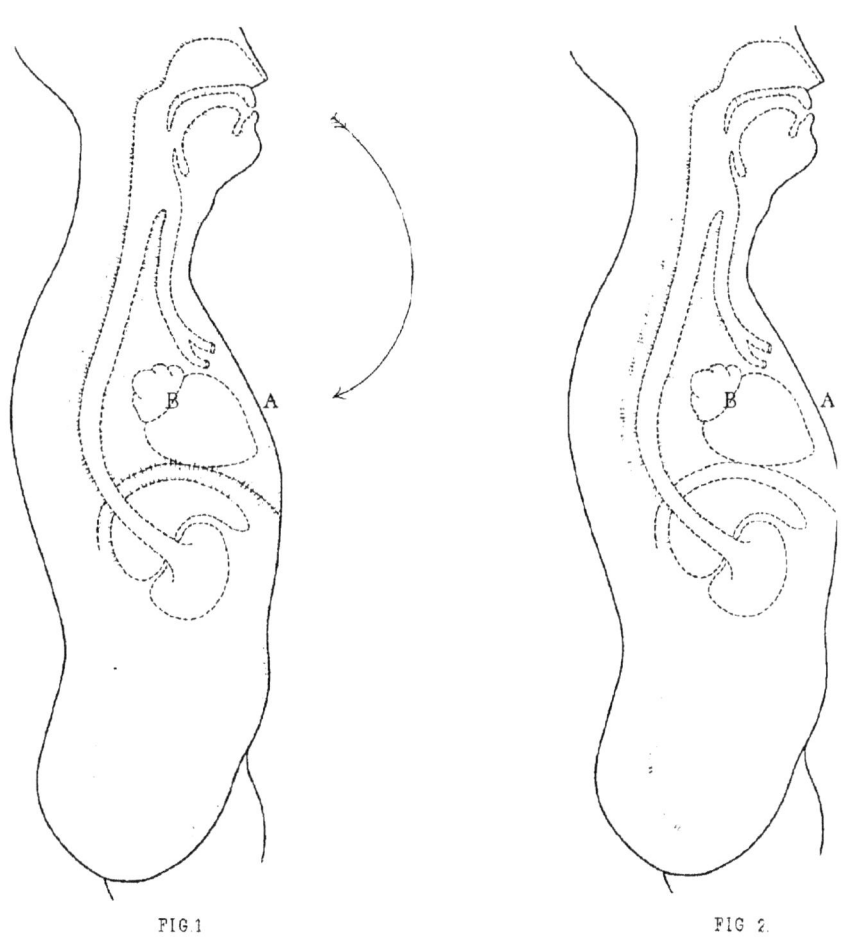

FIG 2.

To face page 142

Indeed, Plato himself draws out the comparison:

Phaed. 112 B καὶ ὥσπερ τῶν ἀναπνεόντων ἀεὶ ἐκπνεῖ τε καὶ ἀναπνεῖ ῥέον τὸ πνεῦμα, οὕτω καὶ ἐκεῖ ξυναιωρούμενον τῷ ὑγρῷ τὸ πνεῦμα δεινούς τινας ἀνέμους καὶ ἀμηχάνους παρέχεται καὶ εἰσιὸν καὶ ἐξιόν.

So far the human form. The shapes of the lower animals are similarly proportioned to their degree of intellectual activity. Flighty conceits beget wings. Indulgence of emotion and appetite distorts the spherical cranium and increases the number of earthly props. Lower passions trail the body in the dust, or—δίκην ἀμαθίας ἐσχάτης ἐσχάτας οἰκήσεις εἰληχότων—plunge it into the impurities of subaqueous life.

Moreover, just as the differing grades of soul's intelligence were accompanied by differing grades of εὐδαιμονία, so the approximation to cosmic sphericity entails an approximation to perfect beauty. The εὔκυκλον σῶμα of a star is λαμπρότατον ἰδεῖν τε κάλλιστον ... κόσμος ἀληθινός (*Tim.* 40 A). Other particulars reach a positive or comparative degree, according to the rank of their corresponding Idea and their own conformity to it. In fact, all natural products are more or less beautiful since they are more or less accurate copies of Ideal types:

Tim 28 A ὅτου μὲν οὖν ἂν ὁ δημιουργὸς πρὸς τὸ κατὰ ταὐτὰ ἔχον βλέπων ἀεί, τοιούτῳ τινὶ προσχρώμενος παραδείγματι, τὴν ἰδέαν καὶ δύναμιν αὐτοῦ ἀπεργάζηται, καλὸν ἐξ ἀνάγκης οὕτως ἀποτελεῖσθαι πᾶν.

Tim 30 A λογισάμενος οὖν εὕρισκεν ἐκ τῶν κατὰ φύσιν ὁρατῶν οὐδὲν ἀνόητον τοῦ νοῦν ἔχοντος ὅλον ὅλου κάλλιον ἔσεσθαί ποτε ἔργον.

In a word, Plato looks upon beauty as the visible manifestation of that goodness which is the essential attribute of mental activity:

Tim. 87 C πᾶν δὴ τὸ ἀγαθὸν καλόν.

Herein he outstrips contemporary art, which, while carrying to completion the principle of unity in variety, omitted that other necessary feature of beauty, *viz.* expressiveness. We may surely regard Plato's fusion of the two, a fusion ultimately derived from his identification of τὸ ἓν with τἀγαθόν, as a distinct anticipation of the modern aesthetic judgment.

Our examination of the human τέλος in its twofold application—to soul and to body—has brought before us in clear relief the conception of the individual as a microcosm, of the universe as a macrocosm. In using these terms I do not necessarily imply that the former resembles the latter in the important respect of being an animal comprising other animals, but merely that the individual is a miniature—a better or worse copy of Mind as it passes into cosmic existence. At the same time I may point out that, just as the opening sections of the *Timaeus* reassert the valid parts of the

Republic, so the triple division of the soul in *Tim.* 69 C *seq.* recalls the threefold simile of *Rep.* 588 B *seq.* and suggests the image of a man containing diverse animal natures[117] within himself:—

The Timaeus.		The Republic.
τὸ θεῖον		= ἰδέα ἀνθρώπου (588 D).
θνητὸν εἶδος ψυχῆς	ἄμεινον	= ἰδέα λέοντος (588 D, cp. 590 B ἀντὶ λέοντος πίθηκον γίγνεσθαι)
	χεῖρον	= ἰδέα θηρίου ποικίλου καὶ πολυκεφάλου (588 C).

This may help to explain the "curious quasi-personification of sexual impulse" in *Tim.* 91 A *seq.* For if the various mental states of the individual stand to him in somewhat the same relation as the Ideal ζῷα to the cosmic ζῷον, it is legitimate to use the phrase ζῷον ἔμψυχον of such a definite state as that indicated by the passage in question. The expression ζῷον ἐπιθυμητικὸν ἐνὸν τῆς παιδοποιίας (*Tim.* 91 C) is to my mind a distinct reminiscence of the πολυκέφαλον θρέμμα which in the *Republic* symbolises τὸ ἐπιθυμητικόν: cp. *e.g.* the drift of *Rep.* 590 A—

---

[117] Cp. also the ξυμφύτος δύναμις ὑποπτέρου ζεύγους τε καὶ ἡνιόχου of *Phaedrus* 246 A.

Οὐκοῦν καὶ τὸ ἀκολασταίνειν οἴει διὰ τοιαῦτα πάλαι ψέγεσθαι, ὅτι ἀνίεται ἐν τῷ τοιούτῳ τὸ δεινὸν τὸ μέγα ἐκεῖνο καὶ πολυειδὲς θρέμμα πέρα τοῦ δέοντος ;

with *Tim.* 91 B—

ἀπειθές τε καὶ αὐτοκρατὲς γεγονός, οἷον ζῶον ἀνυπήκοον τοῦ λόγου, πάντων δι' ἐπιθυμίας οἰστρώδεις ἐπιχειρεῖ κρατεῖν.

It remains to investigate one further result traceable to the law of correspondence between ψυχὴ and σῶμα—namely, the belief in *Metempsychosis*. I do not hold with Mr. Archer-Hind[118] that such a belief "has no essential connexion with the Platonic ontology." For if the localised activity of a given νοητὸν ζῶον attains that degree of excellence which is the external manifestation of the next higher ζῶον, or sinks to that degree which marks the next lower ζῶον, the particular shape under which the said activity was seen must of necessity undergo a corresponding change. To take an example. The Ideal being Man on the plane of sensation perceives himself as a diverse multiplicity of men. One member of this multiplicity —say, Orpheus—is apprehended as possessing poetic genius. When his particular form perishes, a compensating form is bound to appear somewhere within

---

[118] Ed. *Tim.* p. 344 n.

the limits of the cosmic ζῶον. And since transmigration is ever towards τὸ ὅμοιον—

Laws 904 E κακίω μὲν γιγνόμενον πρὸς τὰς κακίους ψυχάς, ἀμείνω δὲ πρὸς τὰς ἀμείνους πορευόμενον[119]—

the new form will appear in the presentations of that Idea which is the paradeigm of the acquired qualities,— say, the Idea of Swan. What has happened is this The Idea of Man has not become the Idea of Swan; for every Idea is an eternal being οὔτε εἰς ἑαυτὸ εἰσδεχόμενον ἄλλο ἄλλοθεν οὔτε αὐτὸ εἰς ἄλλο ποι ἰόν (*Tim.* 52 A). But one ἐξιὸν of Man has vanished and one εἰσιὸν of Swan appeared *in virtue of the fact that the Ideal series is the unitary Mind existent as a plurality.*

But, it will be asked, if the body is such an infallible index of the soul, why do not acquired characteristics gradually display themselves in form and features? How comes it that Horace's fancy is not a commonplace fact?—

> "Iam iam residunt cruribus asperae
> pelles, et album mutor in alitem
> superne, nascunturque leves
> per digitos humerosque plumae."

---

[119] Stobaeus *Ecl.* I. xlix. 60 (Porphurios) ed. Wachsmuth I. p. 445, 23 observes that, according to Plato, the soul ἐν ταῖς λεγομέναις φθοραῖς καὶ τελευταῖς μεταβολὴν ἴσχει καὶ μετακόσμησιν εἰς ἕτερα σωμάτων εἴδη, καθ' ἡδονὴν διώκουσα τὸ πρόσφορον καὶ οἰκεῖον ὁμοιότητι καὶ συνηθείᾳ βίου διαίτης.

It is not a satisfactory answer to this question to reply that the natural kinds are permanent types between which no hybrid means may be inserted, and that the species of the individual is determined by the preponderance of his characteristics. For, once allow that the soul as passively apprehended on the level of sense-perception *is* the body, and it follows that all traits whether they preponderate or not must, so far as they are apprehended, take shape as corporeal deviations. The truer reason is, I take it, that during a man's life-time certain restrictions are laid upon him by the society and influence of his fellowmen, which prevent him from rising or sinking to any very marked extent.[120] But in τὸ ἐξαίφνης, the moment of transition which we call death, the individual soul is not distinguished from the idea[121]: βούλησις therefore comes into play; and, the limitations of humanity being removed, that particular fraction of the entire Mind leaps into sudden realisation of faculties towards which it had previously felt but an incipient tendency.

---

[120] In *Tim.* 76 E he has the rudiments of a bird's talons, not the feathers and beak.

[121] Cp. Stob. *Ecl.* i. xlix. 6 (Hermes) ed. Wachsmuth i. p. 324, 5 ψυχὴ τοίνυν ἐστὶν ἀΐδιος νοητικὴ οὐσία ... ἀπαλλαγεῖσα δὲ τοῦ φυσικοῦ σώματος, αὐτὴ καθ' αὑτὴν μένει, αὐτὴ ἑαυτῆς οὖσα ἐν τῷ νοητῷ κόσμῳ ... καὶ ἡ κατ' οὐσίαν (κίνησις) ἐστὶν αὐτεξούσιος.

Other questions relative to this transition suggest themselves It is brought about, according to the *Timaeus*, by a failure of bodily conditions, a relaxation of the bonds by which we are bound to a certain portion of the ὑποδοχή. Accident or disease or mere old age may so disorder or dislocate the complex of elemental triangles, which make up the material of a man's members, that it becomes no longer a fit tenement for him It has sometimes been held that, in Plato's theory, the molecular angles are dulled and blunted by the wear and tear of life till they can no longer retain the soul. This, I think, is an inexact statement of the case. For (1) if triangulation is the expression of a law, we should not expect the triangles ever to be "warped" or malformed. When pressure is applied, no distortion or "shearing" takes place; they simply crystallise into double the number of sides. The octahedron does not become two *four*-sided pyramids, as it would if a model were cut with a knife, but two *three*-sided pyramids or tetrahedra (*Tim.* 56 D). Again, (2) Plato himself explains καινὰ τρίγωνα to mean ἰσχυρὰν τὴν ξύγκλεισιν αὐτῶν πρὸς ἄλληλα κεκτημένα (*Tim.* 81 B), that is, triangles whose hamation is as yet unimpaired. Hence in 81 C the παλαιότερα καὶ ἀσθενέστερα must be those which are no longer so securely interlocked; and in 73 B ἀστραβῆ will denote the opposite of στραβός, "dislocated." Agreeably to this in 81 C we have the phrase ἡ ῥίζα τῶν τριγώνων χαλᾷ, a double metaphor intended to recall the wording of 73 B:

τούτοις ξύμπασιν ἀρχὴ μὲν ἡ τοῦ μυελοῦ γένεσις· οἱ γὰρ τοῦ βίου δεσμοὶ τῆς ψυχῆς τῷ σώματι ξυνδουμένης ἐν τούτῳ διαδούμενοι κατερρίζουν[122] τὸ θνητὸν γένος.

Thus 81 C declares that, when the triangles of the spinal chord are loosed, φθίνει πᾶν ζῶον: and 81 D adds that, when the same triangles give way altogether, then death follows.

But if death ushers in the sudden transpeciation that I have described, what enables the dead body to retain the lineaments of humanity? How is the σῶμα ταριχευθέν (*Phaedo* 80 C) explicable on the Idealist hypothesis? Again I would refer to the distinction already drawn between the matter and the shape of our bodies. At the moment of death the soul's activity ceases to impress with its appropriate shape that portion of the ὑποδοχή to which it has hitherto been confined, and begins to imprint another portion of the same susceptible medium with new-born outlines. Nevertheless the previous portion is left with a certain definite arrangement of triangles, which naturally subsists till it is dissipated by other forces: this arrangement of inanimate matter—the corpse—is neither soul nor body (though it may popularly be

---

[122] Cp. *ibid.* 73 C σπέρμα ... ἄρουραν, 84 B τῶν ῥιζῶν, 86 C δένδρον.

termed the latter), but a mere congeries of elemental triangles [123], part and parcel of the cosmic ὑποδοχὴ to whose store-house it has been returned. Sokrates may say with more truth than ever:

Phaedo 115 D οὐκέτι ὑμῖν παραμενῶ, ἀλλ' οἰχήσομαι ἀπιὼν εἰς μακάρων δή τινας εὐδαιμονίας.

For the soul escapes; and the bodily form—though not the matter which it once impressed—attends its flight.[124]

Reappearance involves change of place:

Laws 904 C μεταβάλλοντα δὲ φέρεται κατὰ τὴν τῆς εἱμαρμένης τάξιν καὶ νόμον. σμικρότερα μὲν τῶν ἠθῶν μεταβάλλοντα ἐλάττω κατὰ τὸ τῆς χώρας ἐπίπεδον μεταπορεύεται, πλείω δὲ καὶ ἀδικώτερα μεταπεσόντα εἰς βάθος τά τε κάτω λεγόμενα τῶν τόπων.

In other words, the supreme Mind transforms and transports individual souls according to their deserts—

Laws 903 D ἐπεὶ δὲ ἀεὶ ψυχὴ συντεταγμένη σώματι τοτὲ μὲν ἄλλῳ, τοτὲ δὲ ἄλλῳ, μεταβάλλει παντοίας μεταβολὰς δι' ἑαυτὴν ἢ δι' ἑτέραν ψυχήν,

---

[123] The same explanation must be given of all artificial objects—the "house" and "ring"—which are not ὁμοιώματα of Ideas but collocations of inert material.

[124] Alexis *Olympiod. frag. com.* ed. Meineke iii. 455 σῶμα μὲν ἐμοῦ τὸ θνητὸν αὖον ἐγένετο, | τὸ δ' ἀθάνατον ἐξῆρε πρὸς τὸν ἀέρα. | ταῦτ' οὐ σχολῇ Πλάτωνος;

> οὐδὲν ἄλλο ἔργον τῷ πεττευτῇ λείπεται πλὴν μετατιθέναι τὸ μὲν ἄμεινον γιγνόμενον ἦθος εἰς βελτίω τόπον, χεῖρον δὲ εἰς τὸν χείρονα, κατὰ τὸ πρέπον αὐτῶν ἕκαστον—

so that particular life is justly said to depend on the supreme ζῷον:

> *Tim.* 89 B κατ' αὐτὸ τὸ ζῷον εἱμαρμένον ἕκαστον ἔχον τὸν βίον φύεται, χωρὶς τῶν ἐξ ἀνάγκης παθημάτων.

Thus in the last resort we come back to the θεὸς θεῶν, and have warrant for describing Plato's ethical theory as the moral synthesis of a metaphysical analysis, the return of Unity towards itself,—a process that is discrete rather than continuous, inasmuch as the ἄπειρα journey towards the ἕν through the several stages of the πολλά.

INDEX LOCORUM

	PAGE
Alex. *de anim.* ed. Bruns p. 85, 20	7 *n*
in Arist. Met. ed. Hayduck p. 92, 19, 22	7 *n*
— p. 670, 27	3 *n*
— p. 700, 27	45
— p. 709, 28 ff	110
— p. 709, 33	110
— p. 721, 31	110
— p. 731, 16	39 *n*
Alexis *Olympiod.* frag. com. ed. Meineke iii. 455	151 *n*
Archilochus 3. 4	105 *n*
Archytas in *frag. phil. Gr.* ed. Mullach i. 565	23 *n*
Arist. *de an. gen.* B. 3. 736 *b* 27	110
de caelo B. 12. 292 *b* 32	110
de mundo 2. 391 *b* 14—19	110
de part. an. A. 1. 642 *a* 32	62 *n*
— — 5. 645 *a* 4	110
— Δ. 10. 686 *a* 28	110
Eth. Eud. H. 12. 1245 *b* 16	109
— — 14. 1248 *a* 27	111
Eth. Nic. Z. 7. 1141 *a* 34	110
— H. 14. 1153 *b* 32	109 *n*
— K. 7. 1177 *a* 16	111
frag. 46. 1483 *a* 27	109
— 184. 1510 *a* 4	18 *n*
— 184. 1510 *a* 14	34
— 187. 1511 *a* 43	111
— apud Philoponum	46
Met. A. 6. 987 *b* 10	78
— — 6. 987 *b* 10	78
— — 6 987 *b* 10	103 *n*
— — 6. 988 *a* 2	78
Arist. *Met.* A. 6. 988 *a* 14	74
— — 9. 990 *b* 7	78
— — 9. 990 *b* 13	78
— — 9. 991 *a* 2	78
— — 9. 991 *b* 26	18 *n*
— B. 4. 1001 *b* 23	72
— E. 1. 1026 *a* 18	110
— Z. 14. 1039 *b* 9—16	34
— — 15. 1040 *a* 25	91
— — 16. 1040 *b* 12	73
— — 16. 1040 *b* 29	78
— K. 9. 1066 *a* 10	73
— Λ 3. 1070 *a* 26	23 *n*
— — 7. 1072 *b* 18—30	109
— — 7. 1072 *b* 20	14
— — 7. 1073 *a* 11	19 *n*
— — 8. 1073 *a* 16	45
— — 8. 1073 *a* 20	44
— — 8. 1074 *a* 30	110
— — 8. 1074 *b* 8—14	110
— — 8. 1074 *b* 16	110
— — 9. 1074 *b* 33	80
— — 9. 1074 *b* 35 ff	117 *n*
— — 9. 1075 *a* 3	14
— — 10. 1075 *a* 34	74
— M. 2. 1077 *a* 24	38
— — 2. 1077 *a* 29	49 *n*
— — 4. 1079 *a* 2	78
— — 4. 1079 *a* 9	78
— — 4. 1079 *a* 25	78
— — 4. 1079 *a* 32	78
— — 6. 1080 *b* 12	126
— — 7. 1081 *b* 31	28
— — 7. 1081 *b* 35 ff	79 *n*
— — 7. 1082 *b* 32	133
— — 8. 1083 *a* 9	18 *n*
— — 8. 1084 *a* 12	44
— — 8. 1084 *a* 29	45

INDEX LOCORUM.

	PAGE
Arist. *Met. M.* 8. 1084 *a* 34	74
— — 9. 1085 *a* 26	34
— — 9. 1086 *a* 26	27
— *N.* 1. 1087 *b* 4 ff	72
— — 1. 1087 *b* 12	27
— — 1. 1087 *b* 14	41
— — 1. 1088 *a* 15	72
— — 1. 1088 *b* 10	45
— — 1. 1088 *b* 11	46
— — 2. 1088 *b* 32	72
— — 2. 1089 *b* 6 ff	72
— — 4. 1091 *b* 3	27
— — 4. 1091 *b* 19	27
— — 4. 1091 *b* 25— 1092 *a* 5	74
— — 4. 1092 *a* 6	27
— — 5. 1092 *a* 29	72
Phys. A. 9. 192 *a* 14	74
— *B.* 4. 196 *a* 33	110
— *Γ.* 2. 201 *b* 19	72
— — 6. 206 *b* 32	45
— Δ. 2. 209 *b* 33	115
— — 2. 209 *b* 35	78
Pol. B. 5. 1264 *b* 12	98 *n*
— *Γ.* 16. 1287 *a* 28	109
Probl. IH. 7. 917 *a* 39	6 *n*
— ΛΓ. 7. 962 *a* 22	111
— — 9. 962 *a* 35	111
Psych. A. 2. 6. 404 *b* 8	24
— — 2. 7. 404 *b* 16	25 *n*
— — 2. 7. 404 *b* 17	42
— — 2. 7. 404 *b* 24	40 *n*
— — 2. 7. 404 *b* 25	42
— — 2. 17. 405 *a* 32	110
— — 2. 20. 405 *b* 15	26
— — 3. 8. 406 *b* 12	73
— — 3. 11. 406 *b* 25— 23. 407 *b* 26	135
— — 3. 13. 407 *a* 7	5 *n*
— — 3. 15. 407 *a* 29	49 *n*
— — 3. 22—23. 407 *b* 15—24	132
— — 4. 14. 408 *b* 29	19 *n*
— — 4. 14. 408 *b* 29	110
— — 4. 17. 409 *a* 5	49 *n*
— *B.* 8. 10. 420 *b* 19 f	62 *n*
— *Γ.* 4. 4. 429 *a* 27	23 *n*

	PAGE
Arist. *Psych. Γ.* 4. 12. 430 *a* 2	14
— — 5. 1. 430 *a* 17	19 *n*
— — 6. 430 *a* 28	2 *n*
— — 8. 3. 432 *a* 12	7
— — 10. 8. 433 *b* 24	73 *n*
Topica B. 6. 112 *a* 37	108 *n*
— *E.* 6. 136 *b* 7	109
— *Z* 10. 148 *a* 15	96 *n*
— — 10. 148 *a* 20	18 *n*
Chalcidius *in Plat. Tim.* ed. Wrobel p. 200	97 *n*
— p. 202	119 *n*
— p. 203	68 *n*
— p. 204	68 *n*
Cicero *de fin.* 11. 12. 40	111
— *de nat. deor.* i. 13. 34	91 *n*
Clemens *Strom.* V. xiii. 87	108 *n*
— — xiv. 116	109 *n*
— VI. vi. 53	111
Diog. Laert. iii. 12, 13	18 *n*
— 38, 63	124 *n*
— 42, 78	128 *n*
— iv. 2. 1	78 *n*
Dionys. Areop. *de div. nom.* c. 1	2 *n*
Empedocl. ed. Karsten vv. 313, 316, 317	4 *n*
Eur. *Alk.* 965	63 *n*
— *Frag. Trag. adesp.* 421 N.	63 *n*
Hes. *Op.* 129	4 *n*
— *Theog.* 656	4 *n*
Hippolyt. *Ref.* vii. 29	67
Hom. *Od.* 215	4 *n*
— *hymn. Merc.* 80	2 *n*
Horace *Odes* II. xx. 9 ff	147
Niceph. Callist. *H.E.* vol. i. p. 8 B	5 *n*
Oppian *Hal.* iii. 341—370	141 *n*
Parmenides ed. R. & P. vv. 39—40	10
— v. 73	2 *n*
— vv. 94—96	11
Philoponus *in Arist. Phys.* ed. Vitelli p. 352, 20	73 *n*
in Arist. Psych. A. 2. 7. 404 *b* 19	32
— 2. 7. 404 *b* 19	46

INDEX LOCORUM.

	PAGE		PAGE
Philoponus *in Arist. Psych.*		Plato *Parm.* 129 C	75
A. 2. 7. 404 *b* 19	47 *n*	— 129 D	75 *n*
— 2. 7. 404 *b* 21	36	— 130 B	39
— 2. 7. 404 *b* 21	36	— 132 B	11
Plato *Cratylus* 397 C	94 *n*	— 132 B	23 *n*
— 398 B	105 *n*	— 132 B f	1
— 403 C	64 *n*	— 132 B f	12
— 420 D	56 *n*	— 132 B f	15
— 439 E	73	— 132 C	2 *n*
Def. αἴσθησις, νόησις	41	— 132 C	9 *n*
Epinomis 982 B	57 *n*	— 132 D	8
Epist. α' 310 A	120 *n*	— 134 A	10
— ζ' 326 A	120	— 134 B	14
— ζ' 340 C	106	— 134 B	118
Gorg. 514 C	3 *n*	— 134 C	83
— 523 E	104 *n*	— 134 D	96 *n*
Laws 664 B	128	— 134 E	83
— 673 A	126	— 135 C	119
— 716 C	126	— 142 C—143 A	59
— 732 E	129	— 143 A—144 A	60
— 741 A	57 *n*	— 144 A—144 E	60
— 766 A	106	— 144 C	103
— 818 A	57 *n*	— 144 D—E	103
— 828 C	94 *n*	— 144 E—145 A	60
— 886 D	94	— 145 C	103
— 894 A	38	— 145 E—146 A	73
— 894 A	40	— 146 A	69
— 896 A, B	40	— 146 C	69
— 896 B	134	— 155 D	61
— 896 E	24	— 155 D	118
— 897 B	84	— 156 D	104
— 897 B	87	— 157 A	104
— 897 B	106	— 157 B—157 E	61
— 897 B	107	— 157 D, E	61
— 897 C	13	— 157 E—158 C	61
— 897 D	49	— 158 A	82
— 898 A	138 *n*	— 158 B	91
— 899 B	95	— 158 C	28 *n*
— 899 B	107	— 158 C—158 D	61
— 903 D	151	— 164 D	89 *n*
— 904 C	151	*Phaedo* 62 D	83
— 904 E	147	— 67 D	137
— 905 D	83	— 80 A, B	10
— 950 D	94 *n*	— 80 B	2 *n*
Meno 95 E	6	— 80 C	150
Parm. 128 A	16	— 83 B	117
— 129 B	75 *n*	— 102 B—103 A	75

	PAGE		PAGE
Plato *Phaedo* 111 E	142	Plato *Politicus* 273 B	97 n
— 112 B	143	— 273 E	97 n
— 115 D	151	*Protag.* 345 D	57 n
Phaedrus 245 C	40	*Rep* 381 E	123
— 245 E	101 n	— 433 E	128 n
— 246 A	145 n	— 441 D	128 n
— 246 E	84 n	— 415 A	98 n
— 247 C	118	— 445 C	77 n
— 247 C, D	9 n	— 476 A	76
— 247 D	87	— 500 C	125
— 247 E	36	— 500 D	106
— 249 B, C	124	— 511 C, D	117
— 249 C	125	— 523 A—524 D	75
— 253 A	125	— 524 C	117
Philebus 14 C	75	— 524 D—526 B	75
— 14 C—15 C	76	— 525 A	75
— 15 B	76	— 525 E	75
— 15 B	76	— 532 A	35
— 15 D	69	— 580 B, C	128
— 16 C	123	— 588 B f	145
— 16 C—E	76	— 588 C	145
— 16 C—E	76	— 588 D	145
— 16 C—17 A	58	— 588 D	145
— 21 D	117	— 589 E	106
— 22 C	87	— 589 E	107
— 22 C	117	— 590 A	145
— 22 C	117	— 590 B	145
— 28 A—31 A	57	— 596 A	76
— 28 C	117	— 613 B	125
— 28 C	120	*Soph.* 216 B	120
— 29 C	130	— 237 A	6
— 30 A	82	— 237 A	16 n
— 30 C	13	— 237 D	89 n
— 30 C	23 n	— 240 A	70
— 30 D	20	— 244 B, C	12 n
— 30 D	82	— 247 D	100
— 30 D	87	— 247 E	19 n
— 30 D	117	— 248 A	17
— 33 B	106	— 248 A	39
— 58 D	117	— 248 C	17
Politicus 260 D	6	— 248 C	19 n
— 269 D	86	— 248 E	47 n
— 270 A	96	— 249 A	19
— 271 D	88	— 249 A	23 n
— 271 D f	88	— 249 A, B	39
— 272 C	129	— 249 B	23 n
— 272 E	88 n	— 249 B	28 n

INDEX LOCORUM.

	PAGE		PAGE
Plato *Soph.* 249 B, C	39	Plato *Tim.* 30 B	31 *n*
— 249 C	23 *n*	— 30 C	20
— 249 D	19	— 30 C	36
— 249 D	20 *n*	— 30 C	36
— 254 E	69	— 30 C	81
— 258 D	6	— 30 C	82
— 265 C	102	— 30 D	91
— 266 B	97 *n*	— 31 A	20
Symp. 189 E	138	— 31 A	89 *n*
— 190 B	138	— 31 B	36
— 197 E	6	— 31 B	82
— 210 E	104 *n*	— 32 C	64 *n*
Theaet. 156 A	90	— 34 A	138 *n*
— 175 C	128	— 34 A—B	89
— 176 A	67	— 34 B	129
— 176 A, B	125	— 34 B, C	134
— 176 E	107	— 34 B ff	93
— 183 E	16 *n*	— 35 A	26
— 176 E	128	— 35 A	28 *n*
Tim. 27 D	71	— 35 A	65
— 27 D	71	— 35 A	100
— 27 D—29 D	71	— 36 B	93
— 28 A	71	— 36 C	82
— 28 A	72	— 37 A	13
— 28 A	72	— 37 C	87
— 28 A	96	— 37 C	97
— 28 A	143	— 37 C	100 *n*
— 28 B	71	— 37 C, D	37 *n*
— 28 B	72	— 37 D	88
— 29 A	71	— 37 D	114
— 29 A	71	— 38 C	82
— 29 A	71	— 38 E	63
— 29 A	72	— 38 E	93
— 29 A	96	— 39 E	20
— 29 B	72	— 39 E	114
— 29 B	119	— 40 A	138
— 29 C	71	— 40 A	143
— 29 C	71	— 40 B	63
— 29 C	72	— 40 B	93
— 29 E	57	— 41—42	98
— 29 E—30 A	57	— 41 A	64
— 29 E	96	— 41 A	94
— 29 E	126	— 41 A	102
— 30 A	144	— 41 B	63
— 30 B	3 *n*	— 41 B	63
— 30 B	23 *n*	— 41 B	96
		— 41 C	98

	PAGE		PAGE
Plato *Tim.* 41 C	99	Plato *Tim.* 52 A	24
— 41 C	100	— 52 A	71
— 41 C	106 *n*	— 52 A	147
— 41 C	138 *n*	— 52 C	70 *n*
— 41 D	26	— 52 C	80
— 41 D	93	— 52 C	114
— 41 D	103	— 53 A	142
— 41 D—42 E	102	— 53 B	58
— 41 E	124	— 53 B	107 *n*
— 42 A	65	— 56 D	149
— 42 A	66	— 57 E	72
— 42 B	129	— 57 E	139
— 42 C	83	— 63 B ff	142
— 42 D	98	— 64 C	129
— 42 E	70	— 66 B	130
— 42 E	97	— 67 A	130
— 42 E	98	— 68 B	66
— 42 E	138 *n*	— 68 B	117 *n*
— 43 A	131	— 68 D	119 *n*
— 43 D	83	— 68 E	62
— 43 D	134	— 68 E	65
— 44 D	95	— 68 E	90
— 44 D	106	— 68 E	129
— 44 D	138	— 69 B	58
— 44 D	139	— 69 C	96 *n*
— 44 E	95	— 69 C	97
— 45 A	95	— 69 C	98
— 46 C	95	— 69 C	99
— 46 D	23 *n*	— 69 C	101 *n*
— 46 D	117	— 69 C	138 *n*
— 46 E	68	— 69 C f	145
— 47 A	94	— 69 C—D	66
— 47 A	95	— 69 C ff	95
— 47 B	83	— 69 D	106 *n*
— 47 B	95	— 71 A	95
— 47 C	95	— 71 B	118
— 47 C	95	— 71 D	96
— 47 E	55	— 72 D	106 *n*
— 47 E	65	— 72 D	119
— 48 A	63	— 73 A	106
— 48 E	71	— 73 B	134
— 49 A	71	— 73 B	149
— 50 C	131	— 73 B	150
— 50 D	97	— 73 C	139
— 51 B	131 *n*	— 73 C	150 *n*
— 51 D	118 *n*	— 73 D	139
— 51 E	120	— 74 A	73

INDEX LOCORUM.

	PAGE		PAGE
Plato *Tim.* 74 A	139	Plato *Tim.* 90 D	83
— 75 A	66	— 90 D	117 n
— 75 B	96	— 90 D	127
— 75 D	139	— 90 E	36
— 76 E	148 n	— 91 A f	145
— 77 A	66	— 91 B	146
— 77 B	118	— 91 C	145
— 78 A	141	— 91 D—92 B	118
— 78 A—79 E	140	— 91 D—92 B	134
— 78 C	141	— 91 E	83
— 78 E	142	— 91 E	139 n
— 79 B	66	— 92 A	95
— 80 B	130	— 92 B	118
— 80 D	142	— 92 C	90
— 81 A	139	— 92 C	96 n
— 81 B	149	*Tim. Locr.* 94 B	120
— 81 C	149	— — 101 D	140
— 81 C	149	Plotinus *Enn.* II. ix. 8	112 n
— 81 C	150	— v. i. 1	79 n
— 81 D	150	— v. i. 1	111 n
— 81 D—E	130	— v. i. 2	112 n
— 83 A	130	— v. i. 2, 4	112 n
— 84 B	150 n	— v. i. 4	49 n
— 85 A	83	— v. i. 4	112 n
— 86 B	107	— v. i. 4	112 n
— 86 C	150 n	— v. i. 7	112 n
— 86 E	84	— v. i. 8	12 n
— 87 A	83	— v. i. 10	49 n
— 87 A	134	— v. v. 1	49 n
— 87 C	144	— v. ix. 8	79 n
— 87 D	117 n	— vi viii. 18	64 n
— 87 D	126	Plut. *de placit. phil.* i. 10	15
— 87 D	135	— iv. 11	7
— 88 B	83	*Mor.* 691 C	6 n
— 88 B	106	— 1007 F	109 n
— 88 B	137	— 1120 A	6 n
— 88 C	140	Porph. *in Categ.* ed. Busse	
— 88 D	140	p. 91, 14	14
— 89 B	35 n	*Op.* ed. Holsten p.	
— 89 B	37 n	66	6 n
— 89 B	66	*Vit. Plot.* 10	112 n
— 89 B	117 n	Proklos *in Parm.* ed. Cousin	
— 89 B	152	v. 140	7
— 90 A	105	— v. 147	4
— 90 C	105	— v. 148	15
— 90 C	128	— vi. 30	Pref.
— 90 C	129	*The. Plat.* ii. 11. p. 110	92

INDEX LOCORUM.

	PAGE
Proklos *in Tim.* 4 C	37 *n*
— 94 C	112 *n*
— 319 A	54 *n*
Sextus *Math.* viii 286	118 *n*
Simplicius *in Phys. A*, ed. Diels p. 87, 17	12 *n*
— p. 143, 18 ff	12 *n*
— p. 143, 26 ff	79 *n*
— p. 147, 21 ff	79 *n*
— p. 197, 10	67
in Psych. ed. Hayduck p. 10, 33	50 *n*
— p. 28, 11	135
— p. 28, 22	88 *n*
— p. 28, 22 ff	31
— p. 29, 2	47 *n*
— p. 29, 11	26 *n*
— p. 29, 12	43 *n*
— p. 317, 11	118 *n*
Sophonias *de anim. paraph.* ed. Hayduck p. 13, 6	32
— *in Arist. Psych.* ed. Hayduck p. 13, 37	48 *n*
Stob. *Ecl.* I. Pro. 10 (Plutarch) ed. W. 1. p. 22, 5	47 *n*
— I. i. 24 (Philos. Incert.) ed. W. i. p. 31, 5	87 *n*
— I. i. 25 (Porphyry) ed. W. i. p. 31, 8	92 *n*
— I. i. 29*b* (Aetios) ed. W. i. p. 37, 2	108 *n*
Stob. *Ecl.* I. i. 29*b* (Aetios) ed. W. i p. 37, 4	87 *n*
— I. vi. 1*a* (Menander) ed. W. i. p. 83, 20	87 *n*
— I. x. 16*a* (Aetios) ed. W. i p. 127, 19	15
— I. x. 16*a* (Aetios) ed. W. i. p. 127, 20	87 *n*
— I. x. 16*b* (Aetios) ed. W. i p. 128, 14	27 *n*
— I. xii. 1*a* (Aetios) ed. W. i. p. 134, 9	97
— I. xii. 1*a* (Aetios) ed. W. i. p 134, 9 ff	62 *n*
— I. xii. 2*a* (Arius Didymus) ed. W. i. p. 136, 10	82 *n*
— I. xli 1 (Hermes) ed. W. i. p. 277 15	68 *n*
— I. xlix. 6 (Hermes) ed. W. i. p 324, 5	148 *n*
— I. xlix. 60 (Porphyry) ed. W. i. p. 445, 23	147 *n*
— I. lxi. 1 (Hermes) ed. W. i. p. 275, 16	117 *n*
— I. lxi. 1 (Hermes) ed. W. i p. 275, 17	19 *n*
Themistius *in Arist. Psych.* ed. Spengel p. 20	36
— p. 20 ff	32
— p. 21	32 *n*
— p. 21, 17	48 *n*

CPSIA information can be obtained
at www.ICGtesting.com
Printed in the USA
LVHW082206040123
736505LV00003B/18